WHAT'S COOKIN'

FEEDING THE HEART & SOUL ONE MEAL AT A TIME

ERIC PAUL PEARSON

Author, Speaker
&
Life-Long Adventurer

Printed in the United States of America
Published by Eric Paul Pearson
Publisher *eric@thebottomthree.com*

Hardback ISBN: 978-1-7379365-0-3
Paperback ISBN: 978-1-7379365-1-0
eBook ISBN: 978-1-7379365-2-7
Library of Congress Control Number: 2021914330

Dedication – In Memory of
Taion McElveen
11/30/1905 – 8/8/2020

Red Fox – Prestonwood CC, Cary N.C. - Head Chef
Rocky Top Hospitality – Executive Sous Chef
Echelon Experience – Head Chef
The Art Institute – Culinary Arts / Chef Training

On 8/8/2020 Chef McElveen passed away at his residence at the young age of thirty-four years. His humor, his spirit and his amazing cooking will be missed by many.

I reached out to catch up Taion in August of 2020 to reconnect and check on how his lifelong ambition to become a well-known chef was going prior to my return to Cay, North Carolina for the 19th Annual Senior PGA SAS Championship. Unable to receive a response from an email I called the Prestonwood Golf Course and learned of his passing. We all know that feeling, "If only I could talk to him just one more time."

Instead of leaving my experience with Taion in the Appendices of the book under guest chefs as originally planned, I have chosen to dedicate this book in his memory as a tribute to a true and great chef who passed far too soon. This book is about meeting people through a joint love for food and cooking, built upon conversations we had integrated with the food we shared. Therefore, I find it only fitting to have reevaluated my writings and place the memory of Taion at the beginning rather than at the end of my journey.

I am sorry for his personal tragedy while pleased that I was blessed to have met him and was able to have him read and approve this selection in my book prior to his passing. With pleasure I share my experience of meeting a wonderful man with a broad smile for everyone he met and who shared his stories and recipes with me.

Mom's Mac and Cheese to a Restaurant Staple –
by Taion McElveen; October 2019

The second week of every October I drive to Cary, North Carolina and serve as one of the three volunteer Transportation Chairpersons along with current and former Transportation Chairs: Sandy Harwood, Barbara Couchon, Paul Hydcok and the latest addition to the leadership team, Chris Barile. We had served the Senior PGA professionals during the SAS Wildcard Weekend golf event the past five years. This golf challenge is the last event for the senior men to qualify for the Senior PGA Championship. We managed a number of responsibilities including personal pickup of the players at the airport, documentation, inspection and tracking of the rental cars to be distributed to the players upon their arrival, the shuttling of the Golf Channel workers around the course, and transportation for wives and guests of the players throughout the week-long event.

The enjoyment for me other than the opportunity to serve has been the one-on-one conversations with the golfers, their wives and serving as the personal chauffeur the keynote speakers who spoke at the Women's Day event each year. One had to be careful to not control the conversation or interrupt these premiere, yet down to earth athletes whose goal was to maintain their concentration on pursuing their trade. These people were able to compete in the post-prime of life and often stopped by our make-shift office at the Prestonwood Country Club to chat every day during the tournament. They were gracious, shared interesting stories and constantly voiced how appreciative they were of our participation and volunteer efforts.

Once we had picked up all of the players and associates from the staging area housing the seventy-five cars and sixteen vans, had delivered all of the cars and moved the transport vans to the course, our base of operation became the Red Fox Pub next the player's locker room at the Prestonwood Country Club. Our operations ran from 6:00 a.m. to 6:30 p.m. and while the Chairpersons work the entire day, we had three shifts of volunteer transporters who worked three-to-five-hour shifts each day.

SAS Transportation Committee – base of operation
Senior PGA Wildcard Weekend, October 2019

The Red Fox Pub – Prestonwood
Country Club

Head Chef Taion
McElveen

One of my responsibilities each morning was to make sure we had a generous selection of snacks, fruits and coolers filled with water and other nonalcoholic beverages, packed with ice. When I went back in the kitchen one early morning, I was able to meet the kitchen staff and the various chefs responsible for creating selected offerings on and off the pub's menu.

I was most fortunate to meet Taion McElveen, Head Chef for the Red Fox Pub. He had seen me come and go through the kitchen all week and one morning he took the time to stop me and initiated the conversation. We must have talked for almost an hour about our mutual love for food, cooking, where we found our passions, and engorged our souls on the sheer enjoyment in seeing others devour our creations. I asked if he would be willing to share his favorite recipe for this book. Here it is. Another chance meeting and another story added to me experiences. And as you see below, he shared a simple dish he culled from his own mother.

Taion was an experienced Head Chef with a demonstrated history of working in the restaurants industry. He was skilled in Catering, Food & Beverage, Restaurant Management, Menu Development, and Cooking. Strong operations professional with an Associate of Arts and Sciences (AAS) focused in Culinary Arts and Related Services from The Art Institute of Raleigh-Durham.

In his own words:

"Wanting to become a Chef was not by chance but it was my main goal since I knew I could do it for a living. At a young age cooking is something that I have always been around. From watching family members in their own kitchen whip up meals too watching the Food Network after school instead of cartoons. One dish that stands out the most was my mom's mac and cheese; it seems that we had it every weekend for dinner but it will always be the one thing that I remember her teaching me to make. She says the secret was lots of cheese and canned milk, in culinary terms evaporated milk. Her version was simple and true to the meaning of mac and cheese, rich, creamy and baked toasty cheese goodness. But my version with a little culinary upgrade adds a complex cheesiness with several different cheeses and ditalini pasta, which is smaller pasta than her elbow pasta."

Mac and Cheese Ingredients:
2 ea. (8 oz.) bag shredded cheddar cheese
16 oz. American cheese loaf
8 oz. smoked Gouda cheese
8 oz. loaf cream cheese
2 ea. (12 oz.) evaporated milk "can milk"
4 eggs

2 teaspoon dry mustard powder
2 teaspoon garlic powder
2 teaspoon onion powder
2 tablespoons smoked paprika
1 tablespoon salt
1 teaspoon black pepper
2 ea. 16 oz. ditalini pasta

Preparation:

1. In a large pot filled half way with water add 4 tablespoons salt and 1/4 cup oil, bring to a boil. Cook pasta according to package directions.
2. In a saucepot bring evaporated milk to a boil. Reduce heat and whisk in 1 package shredded cheddar cheese (reserving the other for topping), American cheese, cream cheese and Gouda cheese. Whisk until a smooth cheese sauce is formed.
3. Remove from heat; whisk each egg in 1 at a time
4. Add spices and whisk thoroughly
5. Strain pasta then add to cheese sauce. Mix well to coat all noodles.
6. Pour into favorite baking dish and spread remaining cheese atop.
7. Bake 350 for 30 minutes.

Chef Taion McElveen takes on Wall Street
w/ US Foods debut on the Big Board

"In the news: the city that never sleeps got a taste of Raleigh's very own Chef Taion McElveen of Echelon Experiences took on the big city and began cultivating a one-of-a-kind dish for hundreds of hungry brokers on Wall Street; in May of 2016, beneath the skyscrapers of the big apple. That's when US Foods, leading food-service distributor, invited Taion alongside four prominent chefs from across the country, to showcase their culinary expertise in a recreated live restaurant kitchen on Wall Street. Patrons filled the 1.1 km street to celebrate US Foods' public debut on the New York Stock Exchange.

Taion served-up his signature Braised Al Pastor Style Pork Belly with a side of jicama chow-chow and smoky stone-ground grits, topped with guajillo chili sauce. The kick of the pork belly, rubbed with ancho chilies, achiote paste and cumin, was tastefully balanced with the sweet flavor of pineapple — while the grits, prepared with ham stock, heavy cream and liquid smoke, provided a soulful undertone.

Is your mouth watering yet? Ours too. Though you may feel like you missed out on this culinary experience, fear not, you'll find this dish on the menu of Eschelon Experiences newest concept, Bare Bones. Set to open this summer, Taion will serve downtown Raleigh patrons with house-ground burgers, smoked pork, beef ribs, barbecue and more, all topped with his homemade rubs and sauces."

Courtesy of Food & Beverage Magazine

Testimonial by Tim Boyd

Camp Ocean Pines
The site of many adventures in cooking

It is with a great sense of pride and sense of humility that I share with you the impact Eric Pearson has had on my life as well as the lives of the many people around him.

Eric is not your average man. He is larger than life. He is the energy in the room. The shaper of our dreams. The enabler of our success. The passion behind the story. The jokester in the room. The Sherpa to guide us. The coach in our corner. The father figure we needed. He is somehow all of these things at the same time, all the time.

The first time I spoke to Eric was during an interview for acceptance into a leadership program. During that meeting, you could hear the excitement in his voice. Who was this young man from the "West Coast" that wanted to be in his leadership program? Little did I know but that phone call would change the course of my life forever, both professionally and personally.

During the next few years, I built up a very strong connection with Eric. I realized later, I saw him as a strong father figure, one that I sorely missed in my life. He was a mentor and a guide to help me navigate the complex world of careers and growth opportunities. During my time in the program, he taught me the foundations of leadership and after having many philosophical discussions, he helped me find my own interpretation of leadership.

Even after the program completed, Eric continued to be a strong advocate and champion for me in all aspects of my life. He offered me an opportunity to leverage his platform of privilege and gave me the exposure and visibility that I might not have had otherwise to propel my career to the next level. Our philosophical conversations ran deep and they helped me shape the way I think about life to this day. In all of these conversations, he always instilled powerful confidence in me. While I saw a work in progress, he saw potential, which has stayed with me to this day. He also taught me that before we can truly understand who we are as leaders, we need to be able to strip away all the facades and live in the moment. Only then will you be able to start your journey of self-awareness and identify who you are as a leader. Eric's legacy is a testament to the fact that he embodied this ideology. He is forever positive and never seems to let the hardships of life get him down. If you have been fortunate to hear a handful of his stories you would understand that he is a survivor and a fighter and continues to grow tremendously even to this day.

We also shared a love for the outdoors. We enjoyed finding remote places to spend time with our own thoughts, away from distractions. These included many weekends camping trips out to Joshua Tree, where we spent time hiking through the desert sand in search of underground water oases; we used the full moon to search for new animals on night excursions and just exploring mother nature in her purest form. We spent a significant amount of time exploring other Southern California hidden retreats to fulfill our natural curiosity and drive to understand the world around us. One of my favorite trips is when we spent time in the island mountains of the Channel Islands, navigating the island by following the endangered blue foxes and the shadows of the golden Eagles. One day, while out on a long hike, we came across a hidden beach on the far side of the island and I remember realizing just how lucky I was to have someone like Eric to spend time with and to learn from. Eric is young at heart and loves to hang out with those younger than him, as he is always curious to learn, be challenged and to try new things.

In all of these adventures in the deep backcountry, I realized that Eric truly embodied the ideology of servant leadership. Eric's goal in life seems to be to serve those around him. He is a giver who thrives on the positive reactions from others when he performs acts of kindness and generosity. In all of our adventures, he took care of all of the meals and never asked for help. Eric's passion and skillset for cooking was extremely valuable in all of our backpacking camping trips. He definitely took the camp kitchen to a new level! There was nothing he couldn't cook up in the backcountry off of a small 2 burner gas powered stove. Beer can chicken, freshly caught perch, beef jerky, pan drop biscuits, chicken fajitas, streak and eggs … the list goes on and on.

While Eric is passionate about cooking, his giving nature forces him to be self-reliant and self-sufficient. He always tried new recipes and spent time preparing sample batches ahead of time. His goal was to perfect his craft before our next adventure. His ability to improvise on the fly and dedication to preparation is inspiring.

At the heart of it, Eric is a man with a strong foundation, who empowers others, who is self-reliant, overwhelmingly positive and a true practitioner of the servant leadership philosophy. This is why he has been able to create, inspire and sustain such a large legacy of leaders over the years. I am a part of Eric's legacy but I am only one out of thousands. I will be forever grateful Eric and I had the opportunity to spend so much time together and build such a strong bond through our various adventures. Eric has conditioned us to frame our lives around experiences and helping others, to pay our opportunity and success forward and give someone else a chance.

Eric, thank you for letting me be a part of your life and teaching me how to be a better person each and every day. You have inspired me and shaped me into the man I am today more than you know. It is all of your perfectly imperfect skills that have positively influenced the lives of thousands of people who look up to you and will always see you as a guide, mentor, and most importantly a friend.

Inspirational Quotes from Notable Chefs

*"When someone cooks for you, they are saying something.
They are telling you about themselves; where they come from,
who they are, what makes them happy."*
The late Anthony Bourdain

"Cooks, Cook to Nurture People"
Thomas Keller and Wolfgang Puck

*"Performing an act for another human being, cooking for them, is
a form of altruism. And altruism can make people feel happy and
connected to others."*
Julie R. Thomson – Food and Drink Magazine

*"Find something you're passionate about and
keep tremendously interested in it.
You don't have to cook fancy or complicated masterpieces – just good food
from fresh ingredients. The only time to eat diet food is while you're
waiting for the steak to cook"*
Julia Child

*"Take pains with the work: do it carefully. Relish the details. Enjoy
your hunger and remember why you were there."*
Julia Child

*"If you really want to make a friend, go to someone's house and eat with
him… the people who give you their food give you their heart."*
Cesar Chavez

"Food is symbolic of love when words are inadequate."
Alan D. Wolfelt

"If more of us valued food and cheer and song above hoarded gold, it would be a merrier world."
J.R.R. Tolkien

"A recipe has no soul. You as the cook must bring soul to the recipe."
Thomas Keller

"I used to cook because I loved to eat;
now I cook because I love the conversation"
"If I am to change the world, I'll accomplish it one meal at a time"
Eric Paul Pearson

Table of Contents

Foreword by Kathy Binner

"I have always wanted to own and operate a bed and breakfast, so when I retired I did just that. I turned a couple of rooms in our house into guest rooms and applied to our local zoning commission to own the Carraway Guest House Bed and Breakfast. Finally, I was going to use my kitchen, and for more than sorting the mail on the kitchen table.

I decided to offer our guest rooms to a local authors group that was having their annual conference in Columbus, Ohio. Authors were coming in from around the world. Eric Pearson was one of those authors and one of our first guests.

Eric lives fully and feels deeply with a large pinch of humor to keep life flavorful. He immediately became the 'house mom' for all the authors staying with us. His passion is people and his faith… and did I mention cooking with a golf game stirred in for good measure.

He taught me to 'lighten up'! He taught me to not take myself so seriously! "Enjoy the journey", he said, "… and the food!" When Eric announced he was writing this cookbook about feeding the heart and soul, I couldn't wait to find out What's Cookin!

Eric is a complex person, but also a 'down to earth' kind of guy, who loves his beautiful wife Kathy, his amazing family, his devoted pups and his eclectic array of friends. He is compassionate about volunteering, gardening, cooking, his golf game, and a little football thrown in between.

His love for life and people, and his amazing ability to tell a story, is what makes this cookbook something special. He shares stories about his adventures and the wonderful folks he's met as well as the food and recipes he's discovered along the way.

Immerse yourself into *What's Cookin': Feeding the heart and soul through the alimentary canal.* Eric will take you on a journey where you can't wait to get into your own kitchen, try his recipes, and invite family and friends so that you can create your own stories to warm the heart and to feed the soul.

Hailing from Kentucky, close to the Kentucky Bourbon Trail, Eric also taught me that the best cooks drink while cooking, so I will always measure once and drink twice!

This one's for you Eric, my dear friend."

Kathy Binner – Owner / Innkeeper
Carraway Guest House Bed and Breakfast
156 Washington St, Canal Winchester, OH 43110

Acknowledgements

I have a short-list of people I would like to thank for their support and inspiration during the development and writing of this book. Each one had a significant contribution to maintaining my motivation as I developed my cooking skills or kept me focused on producing a well written manuscript. Because each had a unique influence, I have chosen to recognize them in alphabetical order rather than level of contribution, which would be extremely difficult to access.

Tim Boyd

The Ever Professional
Timothy Boyd

This will be short because you will read of several adventures throughout the book where Tim and I shared significant time either in large groups or by ourselves hiking and/or camping. Tim encouraged my experimentation in the kitchen and over an open flame for a number of years as I completed my career at Northrop Grumman during the period in my career that I led recent college graduates through a National Leadership Training Program (LTP). He always encouraged me from his heart and never complained of heartburn.

Mari Estrada

*Mari Estrada and her boys,
Manny & Anthony, 2012*

Pronounced Ma-dee, was my #1 supporter during my journey out west and she became the hotel manager where I spent three years at the Residence Inn in El Segundo, California. I mention her several times in the book because we shared our life experiences about self and family while we both worked hard to make others comfortable and relaxed. She made sure that I had the support to pursue my dream of cooking and became a good friend in the process. You will enjoy reading about her generosity. As I grew my cooking skills she grew her leadership tools and became a well-recognized hotel manager.

Nellie Galaviz

Nellie and her two young children,
Lailah and Isaias 2021

Nellie holds a special place in my heart and was a strong influence during my pursuit of success as a I completed my cooking trials. She was the first person to ask me to step out of my comfort zone and cook ethic dishes, something I had never tried before. She was a young woman who worked at the reception desk of the Residence Inn for three years I watched he grow and mature, appreciated her critique of many meals I delivered to the front-desk staff and her ever present smile attached to a positive attitude. She forced me to pursue and improve every day.

Since I retired in 2014: Nellie got engaged, married, has been promoted to Front Office Manager, and now has one young child plus a new baby in tow. Life goes on for all of, yet the wonderful memories remain.

Erika Pearson Hubbard

Erika Louise & my sweet granddaughter Sophia

Erika is my wonderful daughter who majored in English at The St. Mary's Honors College in Maryland, then completed her Masters in Disability Services at the University of Louisville. Erika's insistence that I needed to pay more attention to my writing and proper sentence structure was critical to getting my message properly documented. She challenged my assumptions and just because I had already published two books, she reminded me that I still had a lot to learn about writing and telling stories, such that the reader would want to hear more from me. We all have something to say, but we must know how to say it or it will never be heard by those who would most benefit. If we are going to pursue anything in life, we must do it with vigor and give it our all. I love you, Babygirl!

Robert Leonard

Retired Colonels drink
Bourbon, smoke cigars and play golf

Robert is a retired Colonel from the United States Army having served an illustrious career in Human Resources. He served our country for twenty-eight-and-a-half years in the Army Medical Service Corp in Kosovo & Iraq, and is a War Veteran. He earned a BBA and an MA in Human Resources. He demonstrates every day that he is a true people person. Thank you for your service and your support.

Like me, Robert loves to cook, also got his start in the Boy Scouts and we both earned the Rank of Eagle in the Boy Scouts of America. There, we share two common bonds.

I was stuck in my writing, couldn't seem to decide how to wrap things up. I was unhappy with my first major edit. Robert offered to be the Beta Reader for my unorganized manuscript and grind through the mess. I felt I still had elements of the book blocking the completion of my manuscript and publication. His honesty and direction helped get me unstuck. He read some horrible sections, some good sections and some incomplete sections. His general comments and brutely honest recommendations made it possible for me to focus and come to the end of this journey and on to the next. Sometimes it takes an independent influence to push each of us over the edge forcing us to make that giant leap to completion. After all, If E.F. Hutton was speaking, we would all be listening.

Bryan Mooring

My love for North Carolina State University keeps me in touch with The Wolfpack Club and recently I stumbled onto a posting by a great graphics artist, Bryan Mooring. I commented on his artwork and somehow, we connected. I won't share Bryan's life-changing story here, not just because it's a difficult one, but it is his to tell. Just know that he is a graphics artist and is recovering from a personal tragedy in his life that has him fighting demons. To be clear, it's not drugs or alcohol, rather he is recovering from an accident that almost took his life; luckily just one leg.

Since we had a connection through the Wolfpack network, I asked Bryan for a favor and in less that twelve hours he created for me the logo and trademark for my personal publishing company. California Dreamer Publishing, LLC is named after my daughter Erika's horse she rode through high school. California Dreamer (we call her Cali) is a Selle François and was a fantastic show jumper.

California Dreamer (Cali) and her colt
by Jeannette Aurmon, Cerulean Farms
ceruleanfarmbedandbreakfast.com

People do things for people just because, with no expectations of anything in return. I hope my gift of friendship and mentorship to Bryan helps set him free from his demons and on his own journey to healing and personal growth.

Carol Schroeder

*A great friend indeed
who bikes 50 miles or more a day*

Carol has been a special friend and supporter throughout much of my work, volunteer, speaking and writing experiences during the past twenty years. As the Director of the Career Center at my Alma Mata, North Carolina State University when I hired many outstanding engineers for Northrop Grumman, Carol provided my unabated access to her staff and aspiring engineering students. I even interviewed engineers who went on to play professional sports instead of becoming engineers. I was fortunate to have hired one talented mechanical engineer who left a budding career as a ballet dancer to become a Radar Engineer.

Carol encouraged me to expand myself by speaking at conferences and joining the Southern Association of Colleges and Employers (SoACE) where I quickly served as a volunteer member of the board of directors for five years. She encouraged me to continue writing and telling my stories and assisted me in editing my last book, *The People You Meet in First Class: When Chance Meetings become Life Changing Conversations.*

Once again, Carol volunteered to be a Beta Reader of this, my third book to catch the obvious errors I missed along the seven-year journey of writing and publishing '*What's Cookin'.*' Thank you, Carol.

Let the Stories be Told

Which came first, the chicken or the egg?

This age-old question is one Scientists today still can't confirm the order. The question was first proposed by Aristotle who was the father of much of the philosophical technique based on inquiry. Aristotle lived from 384 to 322 B.C. and led much of the early development of philosophical thinking we follow today. We shall not debate the evolution of the chicken that certainly evolved from something else, or even propose an opinion whether the chicken or the egg came first. We do know however that the both exist today and all species of chicken hatch from eggs and, most chicken tends to taste like chicken.

Since this is a book of stories about food and the interaction between people through conversation over food, I chose to begin by sharing the following story. I had a one-hour layover in the Charlotte, North Carolina airport one early morning on my way the Los Angeles, California. This occurred shortly after the introduction of the chicken and egg biscuit throughout the United States at the Bojangles restaurant chain. After introducing myself to the manager on duty and mentioning I was researching material for my book on food and people, I asked if I could meet the cooks and watch them prepare this newest creation; the chicken, egg and cheese biscuit. I washed my hands, put on gloves and a mesh hat and off to the kitchen we went.

I felt as if I was Guy Fieri of the Food Channel and his popular show, "Diners, Drive-Ins and Dives". There I was, standing in the back-room kitchen of the Bojangles' restaurant discussing chicken and eggs with the store manager. She was quite knowledgeable and showed me how they ran the breakfast line for all of their offerings and specifically how they cooked and assembled the Chicken, Egg and Cheese biscuit. I am not allowed to share their patented process, only the basics.

The famous Bojangles' chicken, egg and cheese biscuit
It doesn't matter which came first, they all "taste like chicken."

I inquired whether she knew if the chicken or egg came first and how they handled this dilemma on the line. She replied that the corporate training manual had not included a historical or philosophical reference to the chicken and the egg dilemma and it was the corporate office who established that the chicken was placed on the biscuit, then the fried egg, then the cheese and finally the top half of the buttered biscuit. She was confident that it had nothing to do with which came first, rather that it was more efficient to stack the folded scrambled egg on top of the irregular sized battered chicken breast fillet and then add the slice of cheese.

To my surprise the manager offered me two of their chicken egg and cheese biscuits and recommended I prepare them myself. I experimented with two methods. First, I followed the preferred corporate stacking method and then a slight modification by rearranging the order of assembly. I placed the egg down first and stacked the chicken then the egg on top. The only difference in the resultant sandwiches being that the cheese appeared to melt more evenly on the egg than on the chicken. Despite the difference in assembly process, they both tasted the same to me.

Little did I know at the time, but I had just prepared breakfast in the hometown of the original Bojangles' Famous Chicken n' Biscuit's restaurant.

Setting the Table – Dinner etiquette is not an easy thing to master

The theme for one of our Northrop Grumman Offsite Summit weekends hosted at Camp Ocean Pines, Cambria, California was Etiquette for Business, and in one's personal life. An enjoyable yet difficult challenge was administered by one of the Summit Leaders, Dawn Miller, a charter member of The Bottom Three Experiential Leadership Team.

Dawn set each team at a dining table with a complete set of dishes and silverware piled in the middle of the table. The plates, utensils and glasses were stacked up in a random fashion as each team sat around the large table in awe of the sheer amount of dinnerware set in front of them. The participants were instructed to arrange the place settings as they felt most likely to be correct. The session was administered in silence! The team members were allowed to point and gesture to each other and when they all had the same setting, they signaled their accomplishment.

'Not so fast"! The agreed upon settings were wrong, glaringly wrong. Not only wrong once but over and over again. Dawn would only motion with a nod of the head, left to right, right to left and the team proceeded to try again, and again, and again. They would get close and yet make a monumental error and have to start over. Sometimes only one or two place settings were wrong.

Teams received points towards the weekend championship based on how quickly they solved the puzzle. This challenge event was a timed contest and teams received points based on how quickly they solved the riddle. Not a single one of the eight teams completed the exercise in less than thirty minutes, while one team took almost one hour.

Dawn had designed the challenge as a fun exercise around demonstrating proper etiquette and used the knowledge required to properly place and the forks, knives, spoons and glasses to venture through a seven-course meal to demonstrate the difficulty in realizing respectful etiquette around the world. However, an unintended and stronger message was realized by the participants. Etiquette and how we treat others is a difficult task as well and requires hard work plus communication to accomplish and create a sustainable business relationship.

Formal Dinner place setting for a 9-course meal
Photo credit - Gentleman's Gazette

Full Disclosure before we get rolling – My Cooking style and passion for feeding people

I am not a professionally trained chef. I did spend many years honing my cooking skills by negotiating my way around: campfires, Weber® grills, barbeque pits, smokers, and through both small and large kitchens at home and at The Residence Inn; where I spent a significant amount of time in a small studio hotel room. I learned to master my craft working with the availability of many different appliances and kitchen tools. Tools yes, because cooking is an art once you take it seriously, where one develops preferred methods and styles of meal preparations. All accomplished people know that to be successful at any endeavor it requires the proper "tools of the trade." The question begs to be asked, "What's in your toolbox"? Take inventory and start your own legacy in the kitchen today.

Following a tried-and-true recipe from a cookbook or by selecting one from many variations offered on the internet, is an excellent means to learn how to prepare new foods, experience different preparations and cooking methods. The incorporation of additional tools and utensils adds to one's repertoire of cooking skills. More often than not you will experience a fairly successful event. I recommend starting with a proven recipe that has a four or five-star rating, follow the directions and be careful to not stray from the measurements provided. I always had the tendency to stray from the cookbook version of preparing meals and was never too careful with my measurements. I almost always started from someone else's recipe and adapted it as I became more comfortable in the kitchen. I have always been more of "a pinch of this, and a dash of that" style of cook rather than a perfectly measured, ounce of this or a level teaspoon of that. I expect I'll never qualify as a true chef because seldom did my meals turn out exactly the same way it had the previous time or two. I was always adapting to improve the experience.

I discovered during my early exploration that everyone's palate and experiences with food was different. I often modified my creations based on who was coming to dinner, not how I had prepared it the previous time. Most of my family doesn't care much for "heat" created by the use of certain spices in their meats, so they enjoyed a lighter infusion of spices than most of the meals I prepared. My opportunity to prepare spicy food is limited to special guests, however not my ability to create some fantastic hot foods. I have learned to cook such that the heat of the spices does not burn your lips or tongue, rather the preparation allowed the heat to build in the back of your throat, improving the experience. If you can't get it past your tongue, you'll never try it again.

The lack of opportunity to use many different cooking styles in the beginning combined with busy work and travel schedules led me to adapt many of my recipes and led to slow-cooking became a staple in my repertoire.

Some meats do require fast cooking to achieve the desired taste and consistency while others prefer "slow and easy as you go" processes to attain the desired result. The leaner the meat, the more careful one must be in cooking the main course. If you want a sliceable pork roast cook it at a higher temperature for a shorter period of time. If you want that same cut of pork to become shredded for BBQ, then it must be cooked slow with extra juices added to the pot, cooked on low for eight to ten hours and pulled apart with two forks once it is cool enough to the touch. Then you add the extra spices or sauce to create your pork BBQ meal.

Traveling through the Alimentary Canal (definitely not the Panama or Suez)

During the time period in the United States long before it became commonplace for both parents to work outside of the home, families were able to sit together at the dinner table. We always had to say a prayer before we were allowed to eat. Mom or dad would take two to three minutes to bless the food, dad for earning the money, mom for making the dinner, give thanks for all the good of the day and offer prayers for those in need. On and on and on, until often the dinner had cooled off a bit too much for my preference. My personal favorite blessing came from our Uncle Curtis Burton Pearson who was the self-proclaimed comedian in the Pearson family. "Over the teeth & through the gums, watch out stomach here it comes"! It was a simple blessing, yet it properly represented the top end of the alimentary canal fairly well.

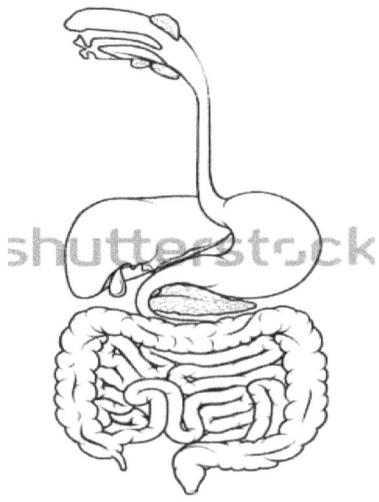

The Human Alimentary Canal

Times have changed significantly since I was a kid grow-ing up in the 1950's and 1960's. Beginning sometime the 1980's most families drifted away from the daily routine of gathering around the dining room table for dinner and conversation. Now we have eat-in kitchens and only the wealthy have formal dining rooms. More families became saddled with both parents having to work and therefore the structure of the family meal, what is cooked and how it is prepared, has changed significantly. The growth of youth sports and other after school clubs created the "car-pool" effect, where everyone was going in different direc-tions. Even if mom and dad were home for dinner, often the children were "on the road." With everyone at practice, games, performances or working out at the gym, life had become so busy that more than not it was deemed a special occasion when the entire family sat down together and carried on a meaningful conversation over a home cooked meal. A crying shame if you were to ask my opinion.

I had studied the realm of Biological Sciences in college and spent a lot of time memorizing the tools and chemistry involved in higher level courses i.e.: Anatomy and Physiology, Physiology of Exercise, Kinesiology and Nutrition. I learned that proper nutrition is critical to the basic survival of life so I took particu-lar care in understanding the digestive process. I also completed nine credit hours in nutrition during my undergraduate studies. Little did I know at the time that the many years of investiga-tion would one day lead to my own discovery of better health and a transformation. I found it necessary to transition from an unhealthy, high of two-hundred-forty-eight pounds, to my stable weight of one-hundred-ninety pounds. If I balloon to 200 pounds I can get back to 190 pounds in two weeks without starving myself.

The alimentary canal includes the mouth, pharynx, esoph-agus, stomach, small intestine, large intestine, and anus. The purpose of the alimentary canal, a.k.a. digestive system, is to ingest food and drink, send it along the pathway to: breakdown, absorption, conversion, distribution of nutrients, storage of fats (this is a good thing), and eventual disposal of the waste products. The food is processed in an intricate manner to break down and distribute the nutrients to the individual cells for sustainment and growth and to remove the solid wastes at the end of the process.

My Personal Journey with Food – In the Beginning (my beginning)

I was born on a cold snowy day, September 17, 1949 in Southern California just north of Los Angeles, in the town of Van Nuys. There were few meteorological records kept back then, but I still have a black and white picture of the snow that arrived that special day in my life. Yes, you read it correctly, we were on the coast of Southern California where the high in September 2017 was 100 degrees Fahrenheit (F), and the low was 60 degrees F when the average for the month was 73 degrees F. It was a special day when I arrived; weighing in at robust 6 lbs. 3 oz.

As all mothers' claim, my mine said I was a beautiful baby and that Angels had played trumpets upon my arrival. Looking back, I would venture a guess that most of them played off-key. Mom said that the snow was just icing on the cake. Mothers do say the most interesting things, mine being no exception. I appeared healthy, had all ten fingers and toes and being on the lighter side of seven pounds at birth I was hungry from the start. Food was definitely in my future. The story mom told several times over the years as the five of us kids grew up was that compared to my siblings, I was the only one to cry all the time. She said I cried for the entire first two weeks of life. I was the second oldest of five children born into the family and we were all breast fed the first year or so. My brother Johnnie arriving one year and two weeks before me was still nurtured on the breast when I showed up, so we had to share mom's dietary offerings. Mom was sure that I was getting enough to eat and feared something else was wrong, because Johnnie had never cried and we ate at the same time every day.

After fourteen sleepless nights and a lot of wailing on my part, mom took me to the pediatrician for my two weeks checkup and asked the doctor what could be wrong with me. He told her that nothing was wrong and suggested perhaps I was just hungrier than my brother, and recommended she take me home and feed me cereal until I quit crying. There you have it, at two weeks of age I was introduced to solid foods and began eating cereal the consistency of oatmeal. I never cried again until my girlfriend broke up with me my sophomore year in college. I did become a tad chubby during that first year of life, a condition that remained with me until my growing through puberty spurt occurred at the age of eighteen. I tried out for the North Carolina State University soccer team, quickly lost twenty-eight pounds as I grew five inches in height during a short three-month period.

I already knew by the age of three (3) that I wanted to become a chef and became a taste tester for anything that was prepared in our kitchen. I discovered quickly how much I loved the texture of foods and dreamed that I too would grow up to someday create my own unique recipes. This book documents my life-long journey that provided me the fuel to accomplish many things throughout my life. By the age of four I was experimenting in our own kitchen and so the stories began.

As a child I held onto two career dreams: 1) to become a successful comedian and, 2) to become a short-order cook. Little did I realize at the time that although both appeared to be great careers, neither was an easy path to profitability that had any chance of carrying me to a financially self-sustaining career. I attempted numerous careers including: lifeguard, paperboy, grocery clerk, ditch-digger, carpenter, athletic coach and teacher. I fell into a path of wandering without purpose and battled extreme challenges at every turn. Somehow, I became a Director Radar Engineering responsible for molding the early careers of many engineers and business employees. All those experiences allowed me in retirement to become an author and I began to share the stories about my experiences of the people I had met along the way starting with my first book published in 2008 and second one in 2017.

A Short History of Cooking – Where it all began (so they say)

I will not document here the entire history of cooking or its deep origins as they are well debated in scientific circles by anthropologists who are far more studied on the subject than I am. Yet, I feel it is important to establish that cooking is a long-standing tradition and it does serve great purpose in cooking meat rather than eating it raw. I'm not sure our distant ancestors knew the benefits at the time but they did embrace if over the years. The discovery of fire and cooking a wooly mammoth over a roasting fire became commonplace; if one could even kill a wooly mammoth.

Don't get me wrong, I take nothing away from those who love steak tartare (raw ground beef) and I definitely eat my share of Sushi (raw fish in rice) and Sashimi (raw fish on rice). Archaeologists Will Roebroeks of Leiden University in the Netherlands and Paola Villa of the University of Colorado Museum found evidence for frequent use of fire by European Neanderthals between 400,000 and 300,000 years ago. Roebroeks and Villa looked at all the data collected at European sites once inhabited by hominids and found no evidence of fire before approximately 400,000 years ago—but plenty after that threshold.

Richard Wrangham, an anthropologist at Harvard University, claims that hominids became people—that is, acquired traits like big brains and dainty jaws—by mastering fire. He placed this development at about 1.8 million years ago. This is an appealing premise no matter who you are. For those who see cooking as morally, culturally, and socially superior to not cooking, it is scientific validation of a worldview: proof that cooking is literally what makes us human.

This hypothesis stems from a few modern observations. When you eat cooked food, you have access to many more calories than if you eat the same amount of raw food. There are two reasons. Our digestive systems can extract more calories from a cooked steak rather than a raw steak, and it takes much less energy to cook and eat a steak than to gnaw on a raw one for hours. Access to cooked food meant a hominid no longer required enormous teeth to break down all that raw meat and roughage into swallowable chunks of a fresh killed meal, nor does it need as robust a digestive system today to process it all. The combination of more calories and less complicated intestines means more energy can be devoted to cogitating—hence *H. erectus*' relatively big brains, which suck up a lot of calories. As evidence for his theory, Wrangham likes to point to the fact that modern-day humans can't thrive on an all-raw diet—raw female foodists tend to stop menstruating, precluding reproduction.

The Joy of sharing food begins at an early age

Since I had become an avid eater at the age of two weeks, it made perfect sense that I discovered my love for eating and cooking at a young age. It was many years however before I realized the power it had in bringing diverse and often total strangers together for a common purpose; partaking of a meal surrounded by meaningful conversation.

The simple offer to share a sandwich with a lonely student in the school lunch room when I was a third grader was my first recollection of my desire to share with others. To share an apple, a pear, half a sandwich, or just some chips; showed me a glimpse into the world of bonding and communication that could be savored throughout one's life. Nothing in common other than a hunger pang is all it required to meet a new soul and have shared simple conversation.

While a few others bullied their way around the lunchroom demanding kids' lunch money and taking their snacks, I had chosen the path of sharing the food I had brought from home. I tried to always remember to bring an extra sandwich and a piece of fruit every day. It was during that time in my life I realized that the power of food and shared conversation opened many doors to relationships I would have otherwise never experienced. We must eat and drink and our mother had always taught us that everyone was welcome at our table. Why not do it over a well-prepared meal and in the comfort of your own home while engaging interesting and different people? Food is an equalizer and a great icebreaker. If a conversation is going bad, just say, "Shut up and eat."

"Oh Brother, Where art Thou?" – Let's talk about early culinary success

I had always enjoyed cooking. That desire must be genetic because my mother was a great Italian cook. She forever claimed that my youngest brother (by fourteen years) Curtis, was the most brilliant child she had birthed and insisted he became a chef a very young age. Mom professed many times that Curtis Harvey Pearson climbed up to the stove and cooked scrambled eggs by himself when he was eighteen months old. I do expect that he could reach the counter top by the age of two and might not have needed to climb on anything to reach the stove. He always was tall, arriving in this world at twenty-six inches in length and topping out at a height of 6'5", perhaps even 6'6" by the time he was fifteen years old and a robust figure at 195 pounds. He played lacrosse, ran track and was the President of his Senior Class.

For years I have continued to challenged Curtis to a family cook-off, though I think he had been intimidated by my proven expertise at splitting, marinating, prepping, building a pit and grilling an entire pig over a home-made grill. He was always bigger, stronger, smarter and better looking than me, but in the kitchen, I am sure I am the master because I practice and perform where he dabbles.

Why are we So Absorbed with Cooking / Eating?

My wife, Kathy, more than once inquired of me, "Eric, why do you spend an hour at the grocery store shopping, an hour and a half to two hours in the kitchen cooking, and then another thirty minutes cleaning up when we sat down and finished the meal in fifteen minutes"? I offered a few of my quick responses and then decided that to be truthful it required some deep thought and a bit of research into my personal motivation. The quick thoughts that ran through my head were:

1. It's always crowded at the restaurants and too noisy to enjoy dinner out,
2. It's raining, snowing, windy … the sun is too bright, it's too cold, I'll have to put clothes on, just to venture outside,"
3. It was a hard day at work, I just want to stay home and not go back out,
4. Don't worry dear, I'll do all the cooking and cleaning, it's easy and I won't make a mess, I promise,
5. I'm convinced my cooking is always better that at the restaurant,
6. Carry-out always seems to arrive cold and loaded with far too many onions and monosodium glutamate (sodium salt).

Obesity on the Rise – By the #'s they don't lie

In 1962 a study revealed that 23% of the people in the United States were determined to be obese. That number has increased steadily to 39.6% in adults the age 20 and older; according to the Center for Disease Control (CDC). The numbers reflect 37.9% of men and 41.1% of women are obese. If we don't face better nutrition through cooking, we are quickly approaching a point where 50% of us will be considered obese in the early 2020's. These evaluations are based on weight in pounds compared to height, and the calculation is stated as Body Mass Index (BMI). A BMI index of 30 or above is considered obese. My current BMI is 24, guess I'm OK at the time of publication.

So, what is causing obesity? The answer appears to be obvious. Study after study has produced conflicting data even though the dilemma has been researched for many years. Nutritionists have been pushing for better living through diet and exercise for decades. The top three reasons for the growth of obesity can be accepted:

1. Eating larger portions,
2. Confusing "Diet" for "Nutrition" and,
3. Inactivity is the new normal.

It therefore seems the easy answer can be summed up in one sentence; "Eat less, live a nutritionally based plan, and get off our butts and go out for a run." Credit, Eric Pearson

Who is Watching- Avalanches of Couch Potatoes are on the rise

We are obsessed with food. Look up the data, I find it unbelievable, it says that as early as 2001, 8 out of 10 people watch cooking shows. We can't seem to get enough of them, yet as a nation we remain obese. According to tv.com they have researched the number of people who watch television shows and as of October 2019:

Top 20 food shows on television

1. Diners, Drive-ins and Dives
2. Chopped (I applied four times ☹)
3. The Pioneer Woman
4. America's Test Kitchen
5. The Rachel Ray Show
6. Bar Rescue
7. Restaurant Impossible
8. MasterChef Junior
9. Good Eats
10. The Best Things I Ever Ate
11. BBQ Pitmasters
12. Hell's Kitchen
13. Trisha's Southern Cooking
14. Food Paradise
15. Barefoot Contessa
16. The Chew
17. Mom's Cooking
18. Dinner: Impossible
19. Mexico: One Plate at A Time
20. Kitchen Nightmare

The list goes on to include the Top 100 food shows, #100 is BBQ with Bobby Flay

It is Not "as easy as pie"

Yes, cooking is difficult. One's first impression of cooking appears that it requires the knowledge of a world traveler, a cupboard full of all the spices from the Orient, pots and pans of many sizes and shapes, the skills of a PhD chemist, the Artistry of Vincent van Gogh, the patience of Mother Teresa and a connection with Father Time. A pinch too much salt creates a disaster that cannot be repaired, too little offers a bland meal that cannot be salvaged. When do you salt: before, during or after you prepare and cook the meal? Some say yes, some say no. How long do you cook it, at what temperature, in what specific vessel, and what's this nonsense about resting a meat dish before you carve it? Over time and through practice and patience one can become an accomplished cook and amaze family and friends at the dinner table. And, it takes significant practice.

If that's not enough of the basics to confuse the average person exposed to the culinary arts, what about the myriad of choices available as cooking methods to prepare that special meal? There are many choices of how to prepare a single meal, but that can be good. Everyone is not able take the time to develop world class chef techniques or purchase every tool, cooking pot and pan available on the market. Most people try a bit of this and a bit of that and become confident in a few methods of preparing meals; then they stick with those types. I have experimented with and offer different methods of preparation of meals that have provided succulent dishes. On most occasions I revert to a small cache of recipes and methods as my regular routine; pulling out the 'specials' when a single guest to large group is expected for a special dinner.

Cooking methods I have used to prepare meals:

Broiling
Baking
Frying
Steaming
Water Bath (Sous Verde)
Roasting
Blanching
Grilling
Salting
Stir Fry
Poaching
Sautéing
Searing
Amandine

Pressure cooking
Anti-griddle
Barbecuing
Boiling
Braising
Browning
Smoking
Curing
Flambé
Hangi (heated rocks buried in a pit)
Infusion
Juicing

My personal favorite is deep-frying,
but that's not a lean cooking method; unless …

Then, we discover there are many different methods of preparing the raw ingredients:

Julienning

Boning
Chiffonade
Chopping
Cubing
Degorging (drawing moisture from vegetables before cooking)

Mincing
Slicing
Dicing
Melting
Pureeing
Creaming
Blending

Knife skills are a plus in the kitchen:
saves time, appearance, and please avoid sliced fingers.

My personal assortment of knives
adorning my retirement kitchen

Another thought before getting started; adding flavor:

Brining	Marinating
Dusting	Rubbing
Salting	Tasting
Dredging	

Tasting the food is required during the preparation process to adjust the flavors, however one must be cautious. Adding too much can ruin a dish because the cooking process infuses the spices into the meats and vegetables. Adding not enough will produce a bland offering.

Cooking with Shrimp –
Ah, So Many Choices, so Many Ways

According to Forrest Gump; "Anyway, like I was sayin', shrimp is the fruit of the sea. You can barbecue it, boil it, broil it, bake it, sauté it. There's uh, shrimp-kabobs, shrimp creole, shrimp gumbo. Pan fried, deep fried, stir-fried. There's pineapple shrimp, lemon shrimp, coconut shrimp, pepper shrimp, shrimp soup, shrimp stew, shrimp salad, shrimp and potatoes, shrimp burger, shrimp sandwich. That - that's about it." *Tom Hanks as Forest Gump (1994)*

How many kinds of shrimp are there? "There are over 300 different species of shrimp and prawns found all over the world. Both can be found in salt water and fresh water, as well as warm or cold bodies of water. They have an average life span of about 5 years." They all start life as males and later become females. - *Chefs Resources – Culinary knowledge for Professional Chefs and Culinarians*

What do shrimp and prawns taste like? There is no definitive flavor which differentiates a shrimp from a prawn. Both shrimp and prawns are similar in regards to their basic flavor profile, with the primary differences in taste and texture arising due to diet, habitat, and region rather than if it's a shrimp or a prawn. However, most chefs agree that like lobster, a cold-water shrimp or prawn is better than their warm water cousins. Cold water shrimp & prawns tend to be sweeter, more tender and succulent. And, as a general rule, wild shrimp/prawns tend to have a richer flavor than farmed shrimp/prawns when compared to same species.

Chefs Resources – Culinary knowledge for Professional Chefs and Culinarian

What is the Nutritional Value of Shrimp/Prawns? In addition to their water content, shrimp are primarily made of protein.

Three ounces of baked or broiled shrimp provides about 20 grams of protein, just a few grams less than that a 3-ounce chicken breast. Each jumbo shrimp provides about 3 grams, and contains very little fat and carbohydrate. Aside from protein, shrimp provide a pretty impressive array of nutrients. Four ounces steamed contains over 100% of the Daily Value for selenium, over 75% for vitamin B12, over 50% for phosphorous and over 30% for choline, copper, and iodine. And while we don't typically think of animal proteins as sources of antioxidants, shrimp contain two types. In addition to being a mineral that plays a role in immunity and thyroid function, selenium is an important antioxidant that helps fight damaging particles called free radicals, which damage cell membranes and DNA, leading to premature aging and disease. Another antioxidant, called astaxanthin, which provides the primary color pigment in shrimp, has been shown to help reduce inflammation, a known trigger of aging and disease.

What kinds of shrimp/prawns are harvested for consumption? Try Gulf, White, Pink, Brown, Coonstripe, Rock, Giant Freshwater prawns, Tiger stripe, Spot prawns, Royal Red (my wife's favorite). If you conduct your own research, you will discover there are many others prepared around the world.

A Blast to the Past – The day it became serious for me – "Pig Picking" at its finest

This reference is to my first attempt at roasting an entire pig. It was orchestrated as the dinner for our entire North Carolina based family reunion held at my sister Jeannette's horse farm in Woodbine, Maryland. Jeannette hosted the event and I prepared an alternative to North Carolina Pig Roast for our extended generation of Pearson's family members from North Carolina. North Carolina, being the home of pork BBQ provided a great challenge to my early developing skills as a back-yard chef.

I built an above ground pit using forty-eight cinder blocks, leaving two openings near the bottom to add wood and provide air-flow. My brother-in-law, Dick Bair, helped me create a large metal rack with wire mesh (non-painted or toxic) and we secured the fresh-killed and brined fifty-pound pig (a small one actually) to the frame, that the pig had been split and been soaked with a Cuban Sour Orange marinade for twenty-four hours in a bathtub full of ice. We encased the pig on top of the fire with a large cover constructed from aluminum foil and carefully flipped the pig at the three-hour mark. After the elapsed time of six hours and fifteen minute we pulled the pig, set it out on a large platter, skin side out and after letting it rest to future absorb its own juices, allowed the family to pick from any sections they preferred.

A slow cooked, roasted Cuban pig is one of the most traditional foods and cooking style from Cuba.

Sour Orange Marinade (Marinado de Naranja Agria)

5 garlic cloves
3 bitter oranges or ¾ cup bottled bitter orange juice
(I use fresh squeezed oranges, lime and lemon juice mixture)
3 tablespoons olive oil

¼ cup finally chopped fresh oregano
1 bay leaf – finally chopped
¼ teaspoon ground cumin
1 teaspoon salt

I doubled the recipe and cut many 1" deep slits throughout the pig on both sides and stuffed chips of peeled garlic in the holes to increase the seasoning saturation inside the pig during the twenty-four-hour soak.

It was such a success that I repeated the magical event for eighty-five young adults at a Leadership Development Summit in Central California where I had constructed two above ground pits and then prepared two whole pigs over a mesquite wood fire with the help of the Camp Chef, and former Hearst Castle Head Chef, Rick Lawson.

Provide me a homemade grill and appropriate music such as; "Light My Fire, Light My Fire, Light My Fire" (Jose Feliciano, 1968) which is one of my favorite songs of all time, and I'll do it again.

The Early Years Set My Passion – The Boy Scout Moto is "Be Prepared"

I honed my early impromptu and experiential cooking skills during my 'formative years' throughout the 1960's as a member of the Boy Scouts of America, Troop 339 in Severna Park, Maryland. We were sponsored by and met weekly at the Woods Memorial Presbyterian Church, throughout the 1960's. As I completed the various skills and tasks in scouts, I eventually earned the highest rank in scouting, Eagle Scout. By this time in my scouting experience, I realized how much I enjoyed cooking over a smoke-filled fire. Rising early every morning, I would stir the ashes and get a blazing fire going while everyone else shivered in their sleeping bags.

My mother was less than thrilled when I returned after these weekend adventures because all of my clothes, sleeping bag and extra equipment smelled like I had survived a forest fire. She had to wash everything twice and then hang my clothes out in the backyard for days to get 'the smoke to clear'.

I won my first cooking contest in 1960 as a Tenderfoot scout against all other members of our troop attending a one week-end hiking and camping trip. We didn't cook any food for this challenge because it was a contest to build the quickest fire sufficient enough to cook a meal. The contest required we build a fire and then use only one match to light it and success required getting three cups of water to a boil the quickest. The time element alone was a challenge, and having only one match to start the fire required that it had to be built properly before striking the match. One shot, if the match went out before your fire was going, you had failed with no chance of recovery.

By the time I had earned the rank of Eagle Scout in 1965 I was given the honor of cooking for the adult staff during quarterly weekend Jamborees. The Cooking merit badge is one of the original 57 badges that a scout could earn when the Boy Scouts began in 1911, and is one of the twenty-one required merit badges to become an Eagle Scout. I am proud to boast that I earned my cooking merit badge early in my scouting career as a Tenderfoot.

Cooking Hiatus during my College Years

I left home for college in 1967 and though my actual time studying was limited due to other pursuits (varsity soccer, girls, alcohol), I was forced to take a two-year hiatus from my culinary development. Winter cooking during that period in history consisted of heating dented cans of soup and corned beef hash that I purchased at a discount from the A&P ® grocery story on Hillsboro Street. I worked part-time at the store and could purchase dented cans and those missing the label for ten to twenty-five cents each. Once, I thought I had scored a large can of boned chicken without a label. Once I opened the can, I discovered I had paid twenty-five cents for a can of tomato juice.

Since the countertop microwave was not yet produced commercially until the 1970's and hotplates were illegal in dorm rooms, my cooking method back then was accomplished by shoving appropriately sized cans between the registers of the steam heating system in the dorm room during the winter months. Several times I forgot to manage my cooking time and had to clean up after exploded cans; not pretty. As an engineering student I learned quickly that the water in the cans boiled and the cans exploded with great force when left too long in my make-shift stove. I compare it to boiling an egg in the microwave today. I learned from those early failures to poke a few holes in the top of the cans, drain some of the juices to allow for expansion and set them upright during the heating process.

I also built a box and frame that enabled me to hang it out the dorm room window that served as my fridge for milk, cheese and perishables during the late Fall through Early Spring (temperature permitting).

When the University Physical Plant turned off the heating system in the spring, out of necessity, my diet changed because with no heat, in-room dining ceased to exist. With the loss of my heat source, I ate a lot of salads, cold cereals and occasionally found enough change to eat at a local home across campus

on Hillsboro Street. This house was an early form of a Bed &
Breakfast with no beds available, that served dinner Monday
through Thursday for $1.25 a plate, where I ate one serving of
meat and all the family style vegetables, bread and sweet tea I
could pack in.

The Mainstay of Fast Food - Burgers and Fries Has Been Around Forever

I was paid $2.00 cash from my Uncle Ray Taylor for each piano I delivered for the Pearson Music Store on Western Boulevard, in Raleigh, North Carolina from 1967 through 1969. I used that money to purchase a meal on the town once or twice a week. More often than not, the event of the week was to make my way to my favorite hamburger joint. The establishment has been there since the 1960's and is still nothing more than hamburgers cooked over charcoal. To stay in training for soccer and later track & field I often ran the six blocks down Hillsboro Street and then across two lanes of traffic, to the other side of the street to the acquire my char-broiled hamburger fix from Char Burgers ® at 618 Hillsboro Street, Raleigh, North Carolina. They haven't changed the store or the menu since I left the North Carolina State University campus after the spring semester of 1969. The building is still the same walk-up, carry-out service grill it was when I first ate there in August of 1967.

This Char Burgers restaurant still exists at its original location since 1959. They have expanded over the years to ten locations in the Raleigh, Durham, and Chapel Hill area. I personally have only eaten at the original one. Creature of habit you might say, or perhaps loyal customer sounds better to me.

I stop to eat at least once every time I return to the N. C. State campus and still walk-up to the carry-out only window. I order my usual: a half-pound hamburger sandwich on a sesame seed bun, a Carolina Packer's red hotdog with chili and onions, a large order of fries and a delicious hand-made chocolate milkshake. "Nothing could be finer than to be in Carolina ..."

"Eight Hamburgers Please" – Perhaps a Mistake in Communication

After taking my leave from North Carolina State in the late spring of 1969, I worked as a carpenter for the summer through the following winter. One day I fell from the roof of the Epps Truck Stop. I was twenty feet up in the air securing the roof trusses. I lost my balance when a gust of wind shoved me leeward and off-balanced I went. Before I realized what was happening, I was falling between the trusses, grabbing everything I could as I made my quick descent to the ground below. I hit the ground with a resounding thud and all of the air escaped from my lungs. I laid there unable to take a breath for what seemed to be a life-time. Finally, I violently sucked in much needed air and began to check my condition. I had escaped with no broken bones, a number of deep scratches on my arms and one heavily bruised ego. Afraid to stand, I crawled to my car, climbed in, rolled the window down and hollered to the job foreman, "Send me my check, I'm going back to college"! After what seemed to be a wake-up call I began the application process to return to college. The following semester I enrolled and attended Anne Arundel Community College (AACC); spring of 1969.

I was asked if I would consider joining the men's outdoor track team. They needed runners and once I agreed to partici-pate, I once again became a "lean mean fighting machine." I was one of only eight members on the track team. There were barely enough of us to even field a team. They needed a quarter-miler, a hurdler, a discus thrower, a javelin thrower and an anchor for the mile relay. I accepted the mission and quickly learned the techniques for these four events I had never even practiced.

For a book about cooking, it wasn't the success of the team or my abilities at competing on the track that made it in this book. I bring up my athletic prowess only because of a meal we had in Rehoboth, Delaware. It occurred after a track meet against the

Salisbury Maryland Community College one sunny Saturday morning.

Our coach, Bruce Springer, a former high jump star at The University of Maryland, College Park owned a beach house in Rehoboth, Delaware. The house was close to our track meet with Salisbury State University so we spent the night at the beach house and drove out to the local Dairy Queen to order carryout dinner. When my meal arrived, the server announced my meal: "Eight hamburgers, two large fries, a large chocolate milkshake and extra ketchup." I quickly corrected him and said, "No I ordered, 'A' hamburger two large fries and the milkshake." Although yes, I had ordered eight because of my ravenous appetite in my late teens through early twenties, it was hilarious to see his face when I repeated that I had only ordered one hamburger. My best friend in those days, Gary Barker, a far better athlete than I ever became, laughed and let the server off the hook by telling him that I had in fact ordered eight hamburgers and would indeed pay for them. Food was cheap back then and the entire meal cost me less than ten dollars. And yes, I ate all eight hamburgers, two large fries and gulped down the chocolate milkshake. I probably should have ordered onion rings while I was at it, but I was a bit short on cash.

To Eat or Not to Eat, That, is the Question

As a sports coach I created my first "Food Intake Modification Plan" (FIMP) also known by many as a diet. This plan was created for my swimmers in 1978 when I served as the head-coach for the Howard County, Maryland YMCA youth swim team. It was developed in preparation for the senior swimmers competing at the National Championship in Ft. Lauderdale, Florida. I learned a couple of important facts about diets, adherence, and their effects on the participants during this period that I have used throughout my own pursuit of attaining the perfect size and shape. We will not waste time here discussing my weight variations that ranged between 152 lbs. at my low in 1982 to my all-time high of 248 lbs. in 2011. I now remain balanced the low 190's mostly by regulating the amount of bread I eat.

Swimmers and long-distance runners, like many other high caliber athletes, burn a significant number of calories while in training. It can be as many as 5,000 – 8,000 calories per day because of the intense workouts, the amount of time they spend in the water coupled with the weight lifting and running programs. When it was time to compete in a major swim meet (State, Regional, and National competitions) the athletes significantly reduce the length and frequency of exercise in order to rest their muscles and recover before a major event. We call this period of the workout plan a 'taper'. During the taper the athlete reduces significantly her workout schedule to experience optimal performance on race days. The body is burning far less calories and the athlete must reduce intake of specific foods and amounts of foods during this period or gain unwanted weight. As a comparison, the average adult burns fifteen calories per pound of body weight to maintain her current weight. A one-hundred-twenty-five-pound adult who exercises moderately would therefore burn 1,875 calories in a normal day. To lose two pounds in a week, she would need to reduce her intake to a daily average of 1,800 calories.

It's not just the total number of calories to consider, rather what kind of calories intake is necessary to maintain or lose weight. One must be careful to manage weight loss to burn calories that is stored fat and to avoid burning muscle. Extreme diets and large sudden weight loss will cause negative effects on one's health, physical condition and athletic performance. Since this isn't book about weight loss per se, I won't go into further detail all that goes into the choice of calories by food type right now. We followed an extensive model.

Rather than become derailed, let's return to the story about the 1978 Howard County, Maryland YMCA National Swim Team's nutrition challenge. To become disciplined and eat properly to perform at maximum capability was their goal. Since this was my first endeavor into creating a nutritional balance during a time of change in a large group exercise routine, I created a single Nutrition Plan for both the young men and young women. They would be competing during the series of competition leading up to and including the National Championships in Ft. Lauderdale; requiring two minor tapers and a last major one.

The Plan was based on a prescription to maintain or slightly decrease one's body mass while going through the series of tapers leading up to the final push for the National Championships. They needed to balance the reduction in caloric intake while maintaining muscle mass for performance efficiency. It required providing food recommendations and when possible complete menu selections. The goal was to select easy to digest and burn carbohydrates and sugars. Too much taper or too many tapers during a short period of time would reduce the gains in performance realized from the previous six months of intensive training. Taper too soon and an athlete's peak performance would occur in practice prior to competition and taper too late, a great performance would happen during the local community swim meet later in the summer where it's not so important.

The Food Intake Modification Plan analysis:

1. The young women took the plan far more serious than the young men.

2. The young women, more often than not, lost weight during the taper.

3. The young men, more often than not, gained weight during the taper.

4. The young women kept strict records of their plan.

5. Only two of twelve of the young men kept any records.

6. Some of the young women lost too much weight due to a generally higher metabolism rate than others and caused adverse results in their performance (great starts and then ran out of gas).

7. The young women were more conscious to the entire process than the young men which created a greater expectation and nervousness during the process.

8. The young women who balanced the taper and rested well, performed at a higher level during the competition than the young men.

9. The young men, having been more relaxed than the young women, broke every swim team record for their age group. However, none rose to the competitive level they might have achieved had they committed to the design methods designed in the taper.

One might conclude from the above observations that in order to run a successful nutritional study, select only young women. In our case study, the young men failed to grasp the context or purpose of eating less and resting more often. It was as simple as paying attention to what they ate. To conduct a successful study with reportable results, the more serious a person approaches her caloric intake balanced by proven nutrition plan, the more regulated and successful she will be in controlling her desired weight. Diet without exercise is not the answer and neither is exercise without proper nutritional balance.

"Roger that" – Convince someone to eat right and perhaps you will save a life

That same year I was honored to be elected the President-Elect of The Southern Association of Colleges and Employers (SoACE) the need to lose weight became a critical decision. One of my dear friends on the Board of Directors was a retired Colonel from the Air Force and Director of University Relations at Southwestern University in Georgetown, Texas.

Roger Young and I both loved the taste of food and freely admitted there wasn't anything cooked we wouldn't eat, or raw for that matter. When out to dinner we always had an appetizer, a large meal and of course a tasty dessert accompanied by a drink or two. We were probably always the last ones to push away from the table when we ate at a buffet.

We had taken a picture together in front of the Sheraton Hotel in Savannah, Georgia during our Board meeting at the site of our conference the following year. Later, when I looked at the picture on my camera, I noticed how much space the two of us filled in the picture; requiring a wide-angle lens. The name of the hotel was hidden by our massive bodies. There we were; me at 248 and Roger at 244 pounds. I was 4" taller and spotted my friend 4 pounds, but we called it even. After all we were both fat and it would seem begging for a stroke. Pictures don't lie. I set a challenge between us to lose weight by our annual member's conference to be held six months later on the Riverwalk in San Antonio, Texas. To ensure neither of us remained on the quest to better health alone, I announced the challenge to our entire organization's membership to see who could lose the most weight. We scheduled a weigh-in at the next conference and posted monthly updates (progress, good or bad) on the association newsletter.

We held an official weigh-in in front of the entire 456 members attending the conference. Roger stepped on the scales first and weighed in at 214 pounds; net loss of 30 pounds in six months. He was smug and beamed from ear to ear at his accomplishment as his self-assuredness rose … he knew he had won. He had also worn very baggy clothes to appear as if he might have lost 50-75 pounds. Appearances can be deceitful. Who won, was far less important to me than seeing my friend and myself become healthy in mind and spirit. His efforts dragged the over-competitive me along the way. At that moment … I knew we were both winners.

I congratulated him on winning but he insisted I get on the scale. Roger said he had to know by how much he had won. As the proof hung in the balance, I slowly stepped on to center stage and shifted my weight onto the scale. It settled in at 212.5 pounds. I sucked in extra air, hoping it would increase my weight, but alas, it was not to be. I had won the competition by 1.5 pounds. The scale did not lie. I was the winner, but was I really the winner? Actually no, let me explain a little further.

It took a half a year after the conference to realize the actual winner had been Roger. Six months to the day after our famous weigh-in, Roger had a major heart-attack and was rushed to the hospital where he remained 'touch and go' for four days. Once he recovered from the life-changing event the doctor told him, "Mr. Young I understand you recently lost thirty pounds. You must know that if you still weighed over 240 pounds today, you wouldn't have survived the heart-attack and we would not be having this conversation because you would be dead."

A simple challenge to inspire others as well as myself to face our personal demons and strive to improve or mental and physical well-being started as a humorous challenge that turned into a critical life-saving event. Feed the conversation, not always the stomach. Better eating leads to a better and much longer life.

Southern Association of Colleges & Employers
9 years of Presidents

The Power of Sharing Food and Conversation with Others

The following story is one example of how having shared a meal with another person opened the door for me to experience an enjoyable conversation with a total stranger. This story about food is borrowed from my last book about people and conversations; *The People You Meet in First Class: When Chance Meetings Become Life Changing Conversations.* I chose to share this story early because rather than it being one about me initiating contact and offering someone a meal, I was the recipient of the kindness of a stranger one early morning.

Sharing With Sheri from Shrewsbury, PA – September 2014

Inside thirty days of the conclusion of my working career, I was tasked to take a last-minute flight from Baltimore, Maryland to San Diego, California. The purpose was for a one-day program review and return to Baltimore the next day. Even with Chairman Elite Status on the airline, you don't always receive 1st Class seat upgrades on cross-country flights. This is expected to happen when flights are booked at the last minute. For one of the few times in the previous five years, I was relegated to sitting in a window seat in the coach section of the airplane. I was facing a four-and-a-half-hour flight and three time zone changes from Phoenix, Arizona to home. The young woman sitting next to me in the center seat rose and walked to the back of the plane shortly before boarding was complete. I began to get my hopes up that the seat would remain empty and there would be much-desired elbow and shoulder room for my long journey home.

However, two minutes later Sheri appeared from the back of the plane and explained that she had given up her aisle seat in the back of the plane to allow the young woman that had been next to me to sit with to her fiancée. Sheri was performing a kind act and here I was dwelling on my wants for expanded space. Shame on me, I learned a couple of valuable lessons that day. Let me continue. It was time for me to put the grumpy Eric away and enjoy the flight.

Once we reached a comfortable cruising altitude, Sheri pulled out an aromatic grilled Panini sandwich and mentioned she hadn't had breakfast because she had to catch an early flight out of Burbank to Phoenix. I responded by saying I hadn't either because I had an early flight out of San Diego and there weren't any places open for me to grab a bite to eat at 4:30 a.m. Sheri offered me half of her sandwich, and though hungry, I politely refused. She insisted twice, yet I held my ground until she said, "I will only eat half and if you don't take the other, I'll just throw it away." Thinking of all the starving children in the world, I sacrificed my honor and graciously devoured the delicious sandwich.

Then Sheri pulled out a bag of chips and anticipating my response said, "If you don't eat half of these, I'll just throw them away." I ate my half of her chips as well. We had a wonderful conversation and to repay Sheri for her kindness I offered her a copy of my first published book, *Ryan's Stories: God's Perfect Child*. I leaned into the window to take a nap and, much to my surprise Sheri had already begun to read the book.

When I awoke from a much-needed snooze, I discovered Sheri had read more than half of the book. Embarrassed, I explained she wasn't supposed to read it in front of me in case she didn't like the book. She smiled, said how wonderful it was and quoted three of the stories that she thought were the most interesting. Would anyone like a copy of my book to read? It will only cost you half a sandwich and half a bag of chips on the next flight if you sit next to me. Thank you, Shari, thank you very much. I learned several lessons that day and made a new friend that I'll most likely never see again, yet I'll have your story forever.

Feed the Troops— It's Your Turn

There was always a lot of active-duty military flowing through Charlotte Douglas International Airport in North Carolina. When I walked past the troops, I tried to thank as many as possible.

I seldom ate in airports but on this day, I had a long layover, was ravenous and had a craving for something with meatballs and marinara. I decided to stop in at the Italian eatery that I had passed up many times previous on my numerous journeys through Terminal C in the Charlotte airport.

In line behind me, there were four young men and a woman all in uniform. They were talking about having just come back from a tour in Iraq and looking forward to getting home to family and friends. They were headed to Ft. Bragg, North Carolina for two weeks of R&R. It had been a long trip with three layovers and they were exhausted and hungry.

I ordered a meatball sub with a large coke, turned to my right and told these 'War-Fighters', "Order anything you want, this meal is on me." The first one looked at the guy behind the counter, pointed at me, and said, "I'll have what he's having." One by one, all five said the same thing: "I'll have what he's having." I explained again they could have anything on the menu they each wanted, yet they each repeated, "No sir, I'm having what you're having."

We sat together for two hours as I listened to their stories during deployment—some scary, some funny—and they all spoke of how proud they were to serve our country. When you see a serviceman or woman in uniform, take the time to say "Thank You." and considering to offer them a bite to eat wouldn't hurt either. These folks sleep outdoors in all kinds of weather and spend time ducking bullets for our protection. A meatball sub and a coke are far better than a leftover MRE (Meal Ready to Eat) field ration.

Is This a Cookbook or a Book about People and food?

Yes, and yes! The idea of this book was born with intent to share my journey to become an accomplished self-taught chef, trained in my own kitchen, while using the opportunity to meet new people, and share my talents. I sought to collaborate on the solutions to the world's problems during these conversations. Each discussion occurred over a meal designed to enhance the pallet and encourage the participants to open wide. Opening not only their mouths to partake of different foods, but also opening their minds to seek discovery, and embrace empathy for people and cultures of which we often have little experience or knowledge.

The body of work in this book is a combination of short stories sharing some of the memorable experiences from the many opportunities I was able to share both my culinary skills with friends and strangers. The importance to me was the conversation that ensued around the location, be it in:

1. A dining room with linins and fancy silverware,
2. sitting on a couch watching a ballgame for the first time,
3. at the countertop where the cooking took place and conversation kept the food from ever making it to the table,
4. around a common dining area of a hotel,
5. surrounding an open fire-pit next to the swimming pool,
6. out in the wilderness under starry skies,
7. and, occasionally in local restaurant to experience the cuisine of a country I had not previously sampled.

I have also shared the evolution of my culinary skills, methods and terminology about cooking to inspire others to discover their own talents and personal experiences through cooking.

My own pursuit of cooking significantly increased my knowledge of human actions and interactions. I quickly embraced the differences and similarities in all of us from different cultures, different countries, and different backgrounds. My knowledge growth was fostered through this passion I had developed for food and through sharing both a meal and conversation with new and diverse "people of the world."

In my previous book titled, *The People You Meet in First Class*, I shared a number of observational highlights of people from different lifestyles and locations around the world. Some only spoke what I assumed to be their native language; however, their actions often spoke far more than any of the words I could not understand. I wonder how those stories might have differed had I had the opportunity to share a meal with them rather than just observing them during a short flight on an airplane or while sitting in an airport terminal?

In this book, I have shared my treasured stories of cultural exchanges made possible through my cooking and reaching out to meet people who were more different than similar to my own appearance and experiences. Some were enlightening and others comical interactions, yet each and every one was a great learning experience for me.

On to Important Stories to be told

Enough of the long ago past, let's fast forward a number of years to the short period in history this book is intended to share. I never lost my dream for comedy; however, it was apparent that my skills in the kitchen far surpassed my attempts at comic relief. Suddenly, I am a two-time published author, and now developing a book about cooking and spanning the divide between people of different backgrounds and philosophies through food and communication. Throughout history warring factions sat at long dinner tables to negotiate truce, set conditions of alignment to avoid wars or to divvy the 'spoils of war'. When we dine together, we share food, words, ideas and beliefs and we discover that we have more similarities than differences that exist between friends and strangers. The intent of these meals is to forge a common bond while healing the world, one relationship at a time. How many decisions were made over a meal and mead at King Arthur's Roundtable?

90 Years of Italian Feasts –
The "life and times" of Chef John Trani

While working in the exciting world of stealth radar development, we had the opportunity to spend several extended periods of time in Los Angeles, Long Beach, San Pedro and San Diego, California. We worked on the early development of some of the most advanced Radar Absorbent Material (RAM) development during the late 1980's and early 1990's. It was an exciting time and we met often with the many members of our support staff who served as our labor pool from a newly formed company called Nova Marine. One particular member of that crew was especially interesting to me due to the fact that he came from a family of chefs and restaurateurs. His name is John Trani, one of the sons of Filippo Trani, who had joined our crew when we began or efforts in Long Beach, California. His story is an interesting one. In 2015 San Pedro, California celebrated 90 years of Italian feasts created by the Trani family at 584 W 9th Street, San Pedro, California 90731, (310)-832-1220.

Four generations of the Trani family had run restaurants that was often served as the hub for celebrities, one of the most famous being Los Angeles Dodgers Manager, Tommy Lasorda. In fact, Mr. Lasorda was the Godfather of John Trani, the same John who worked on our crew in San Diego. Growing up, John worked in the family restaurant while playing baseball through high school and a few years of semi-professional baseball. When our team from Baltimore, Maryland worked on the docks in San Pedro and Long Beach, we had occasionally dined at Trani's, though I had not yet met John.

At this point one might inquire why Chef John would be working as a day-laborer on a ship and a few years later with us on the Naval Base on Coronado Island in San Diego, California. That's the same question I had asked John when I got to know him better. Being in charge of our subcontractor financials and personnel resources, I had the opportunity to meet John and discuss his interests and work performance. He did not seem to have the energy, skills or interest in performing at the high level necessary to complete tasks of cleaning ship's surfaces, applying a mastic adhesive and securing a special material in a tile configuration; all critical to services on the ship.

John was competent enough and completed his tasks, but a light in his eyes never shone and he never exhibited a heartiness in his step. He was one of over 250 members of the Nova Marine crew out of San Pedro who followed us to San Diego who we managed over a three-site, six-year period; San Pedro, Long Beach and the San Diego Naval Base, then back to Long Beach. The background of many of these workers was as diverse as the Los Angeles population itself.

You can only imagine where many of these folks came from. Some were from your normal day-labor pool who had signed on for a long-term assignment, some were ex-cons looking for any semblance of a hard-earned pay-day, some were members of street gangs in Compton and Watts who took the assignment to get out of LA, and other stragglers who came from all walks of life.

One particular gentleman, Wil E. Coyote (name changed to protect me for starters) on the crew had spent a nickel (five years) in Folsom Prison, one of the country's oldest maximum-security prisons in the country that opened in 1880. It was known to be one of the worse prisons in the country with a history of violence and bloody occurrences as recent as 2010 when over 200 inmates rioted. It is located in Represa, California, near Sacramento. This is the same Folsom Prison Johnny Cash made famous after release of his live album, Folsom Prison Blues in 1955. This song and his experience at Folsom Prison changed his life forever when he returned to sing for two live tapings in 1968.

John was having difficulty getting to work and his on-deck supervisor had indicated his work performance had fallen off. I met with John and through our discussion found out more about his personal story. I have already shared his family Italian restaurant business and his tie to Tommy Lasorda so, here is the rest of his story.

John was a family trained chef, grew up in the family business and was known for his skills in the area of fish and seafood. He is credited with bringing fish to the traditional menu at J. Trani's Ristorante. John also shared with me his passion for baseball growing up and his background in cooking and the restaurant business. John related his desire to expand his culinary expertise in a more formal atmosphere than was offered in San Pedro, California. "After all," he said, "how many ways can an Italian cook eggplant"? "I don't know," I responded, "how many"? We both had a loud laugh and he continued to share his story.

I asked several questions and quizzed him on some of his recipes. He definitely knew far more than I would ever earn. He spouted off several recipes, species of fish, preparation techniques and offered a unique style for marinating large pieces of meat. I was dutifully impressed. Thus, the answer to the next question cleared up why such a culinary talent was working as a day-laborer on a Naval Shipyard. The work wasn't easy, it required working ten hours a day, seven days a week. The pay was good, but that couldn't be his reason for coming, otherwise his efforts would have been better.

John said that he had heard through the grapevine that once we completed our demonstration of stealth tile application to reduce the ship's Radar Cross Section (RCS) that our next assignment was going to be coating ships at the Naval Station in Pearl Harbor, on the lagoon of Oahu, Hawaii. His thoughts were that once in Hawaii and our job was complete, he could stay there a few years to train with local chefs in traditional Hawaiian fare and then move to Japan to pick up the culinary secrets of that culture. He wanted to island hop his way through his training experiences. John Trani was tired of pasta dishes with meatballs and wanted to chase his passion for seafood. That's his story and I'm sticking to it.

Sounded like a great plan at the time, however we had no knowledge of considering expanding our efforts to Hawaii or anywhere else and we never went there. We were Radar design engineers developing highly classified state of the art electronic capabilities. Once a technology was proven, we transferred everything to the United States Government for further development and their incorporation into the fleet of ships. The last I heard all those years ago was that the government installations took place back in Long Beach, only five miles from John Trani's home in San Pedro. He had traveled with us over a three-year period only to return to home and to J. Trani's Ristorante.

Historically Speaking –
It Came Upon Many Midnights Clear

As we maneuver our way through the highways and byways of life, we are often challenged with making the most of the situations we face. My greatest detour came from the requirement to travel for business; taking me away from my family, friends and familiar surroundings. One can choose to mull about the distractions, delays, numerous days and nights in strange hotels and towns or we can do something proactive about the experience. All of these distractions can lead to an exhausting and less productive experience while on the road. To make the best of my situation, I embraced the opportunity to meet new people, experienced new locations, engorged myself in other cultures, participated in social activities and initiated discussions that enriched my soul. I hope these interactions accomplished the same for the others who engaged with me as well.

My career in Radar Defense Electronics had become one more of being on the road than in the office. I faced numerous obstacles and choices that led to many of the stories included in this book. This is my third non-fiction book. The stories are true, unembellished and shared in hopes that we might continue to heal our differences by realizing even strangers are far more alike than not. The results are intended to lead to a common ground of communication, understanding and collaboration. That first impression is often the only impression we will ever make with most people we meet.

This book is filled with the power and enjoyment derived from many conversations that arose from my enjoyment of cooking for others and having met diverse people over many years of travel. I have provided some of my favorite recipes of the over two-hundred recipes that I developed during the three-year period in California. I created them as a means of entertaining myself as I delved into self-experimentation of how to cook a variety of ethnic and local foods that were new to my palate.

I painted many an artistic masterpiece in that small kitchen, using a variety of brushes. Instead of paint, my pallet was laden with sugars and spices from around the world, herbs and stocks, catsups and mustards, dried and fresh condiments, and quite often a serious amount of minced garlic. This period of time away from my family became a special journey for me in the kitchen. Through the pursuit of sharing my culinary passions and engagement skills with all friends and strangers who crossed my path, I developed a personal sense of the people around me.

My "family" at The Residence Inn, El Segundo, California
supervisors, desk clerks, maintenance, cleaning personnel, groundskeepers

The predominate setting for my culinary experimentations became The Residence Inn located in EL Segundo, California where I lived ninety-five percent of the time from 2011 to 2014. Yes, my home life suffered from the separation, but I had no choice. At the time I was serving on the Executive Team as the Sector Director of Advanced Program Development and Cross-Sector Relationships for the Northrop Grumman Corporation. I wasn't one for eating out at restaurants, or hanging out in bars partaking of greasy appetizers during Happy Hour. I spent a greater portion of my evenings watching "Chopped" on The Food Channel and cooking small and large dishes in my attempt to replicate the new dishes I observed being created during staged competitions on television.

"Guess Who's Coming to Dinner" – no, not Sidney Poitier; although I wish he had

When I cooked for others, the recipe of choice depended on who was my next dinner guest:

1. Me, myself and I (yes, I often ate alone),
2. The front desk services staff who worked the evening/night shift,
3. The hotel management staff who ran the day–to-day operations,
4. Long-term residents such as myself I had become to know over time,
5. Interesting short-term guest whose aura appeared as if to have their own story to tell,
6. Young engineers in the area who had been in my Leadership Training Program (LTP),
7. Special friends who enjoyed hiking and camping on islands, in the wilderness and desert,
8. Peer Executives who often traveled to California for work,
9. Family who occasionally came to visit,
10. Corporate partners who worked in my West Coast office,
11. The entire hotel management and cleaning staff (45 women and a couple of guys).

"Just Dropped In to See What Condition My Condition was In"- Mickey Newbury 1968

After several previous careers and a growing presence flying around the United States for business, I had accepted the special assignment in EL Segundo, California in the fall of 2011. That short-term position resulted in my spending 95% of my time over a three-year period living in a hotel studio. For the first time in twenty-five years, I was away from my family and the comforts of home for extended periods of time. Suddenly my residence had become 464 square feet that included the bathroom, the bed, the living room and the kitchen. My bed looked into in the living room without a door and the open-air layout included the smallest kitchen possible yet still be classified as a full kitchen. Most of the studio rooms only had a small cooktop for preparing meals. The Residence Inn hotel management and staff always ensured that I was booked into a room that included a full oven in the front of the main building. Once they got to know my schedule and ate my food, they always provided me one of two specific rooms for the last two years of my stay in EL Segundo.

Another dilemma had befallen me that became a significant element of this new journey in life. After nearly six years of significant travel and time on the road my weight had ballooned back to two-hundred-forty-eight pounds on my 6'2.5" frame. I presented the appearance of a slightly overweight former football player when in fact I had played soccer in college some forty-four years previous at one-hundred-and-sixty-seven pounds. Back in college I was in shape. At that time in my life, I sported a resting pulse of forty-four beats per minute and heathy blood pressure of 110/66. Once I reached my maximum girth potential and by being out of shape, my blood pressure was steady at 145/110, my heart rate seventy-four beats a minute and I often found myself short of breath. On many occasions I searched for the closest parking space wherever I went. I had become lazy, fat and out of shape. While in denial, my weight grew over the years I would say I had small bones when I was young and as I argued that somehow, my bones, not me, had gotten bigger and heavier.

Without realizing what had happened, I had gradually slipped into middle-age and a relatively unfit health condition. I pretended to be unaware of my growing stature until one day I looked into the mirror and discovered a fat man looking back at me. I barley recognized the reflection. OMG! It was me and definitely the time had come to change my lifestyle. Here I was just three years from retirement and as unhealthy as one could be without a legitimate physical or mental condition on which to blame my current health status. If I wanted to remain alive long-term to enjoy my impending retirement, it was time for action.

I decided to make significant lifestyle changes through a regular routine of diet and exercise while developing and incorporating lean cooking methods and improved eating habits as a daily routine. I started by eliminating all bread options, candy and anything full of sugar; except for my home-brewed southern sweet tea. Eliminating soft drinks from my diet was the toughest choice I made. I went from two sixteen-ounce cokes a day to two twelve ounce cans to one twelve ounce can and finally no coke.

Location, Location, Location

I knew that I was going to be stationed on the West Coast for a long time. Therefore, if I was going to make a serious effort to lose that fat man who stared back at me every time I peered into the mirror, it would require a hotel that had appropriate cooking facilities. After all things considered, I chose the Residence Inn by Marriott on East El Segundo Boulevard. It was only 2.7 miles from the Los Angeles International Airport and less than one mile from my office at work.

Before I took my first trip to El Segundo, I completed some research and discovered a short three blocks from my new California office was a Residence Inn by Marriott. I called the hotel and spoke with the Director of Marketing, Mari Estrada. Mari is pronounced Ma-Dee. Although they were not an approved vendor for Northrop Grumman corporate housing, she agreed to provide me the local Per Diem rate for my first three-week stay. Mari promised to contact Marriott corporate folks and inquire as to adding us to their preferred contractors. The long story short is everything worked out and I spent all of my time during the next three years living at The Residence Inn, EL Segundo, California. Here is where I further developed my communication and culinary skills while making many new friends on staff, watching people come and go, and inspiring me in the development of *What's Cookin'*.

During the initial three months of my deployment on the left coast, I had tried out the different room options available and locations throughout the hotel: Studio with a cook top, studio with a full oven, one bedroom with an oven and one bedroom with a cook top. It worked out that the best option for me was to stay in one of the larger corner studios with a full oven on the third floor of the main building in the front corner of the hotel. That option offered me the largest living space possible with the best cooking facilities available. It was also far enough from the elevator that it was more convenient for me to climb the stairs than walk the extra distance to use the elevator. The room choice afforded me a built-in exercise routine. I started by slowly walking the stairs and over time as I began to lose weight and got into shape, I would race up the stairs taking two and three steps at a time.

My goal at the beginning of this journey was to eat healthier, begin an exercise routine, and lose forever as much weight possible. This became a significant change of course since in the previous six years of travel I managed to eat my way into my current situation. I initially spent a lot of time alone and challenged myself to replicate the many twenty-minute meals the contestants were required to prepare on the Food Channels hit show, *Chopped*. Often my own fridge appeared to be a mystery of choices and I too began to create something from a mixed bag of nothings. Over time, as I began to get to know the hotel staff and some of the other long-term residents, I started to engage them in conversation over the many meals I created and prepared to share with them.

The First Trip to the Grocery Store – Let the Experiments Begin

After flying all morning from the east coast, setting up my new office checking into the hotel, I decided to venture out to the grocery store for my first set of purchases. The local store in the area was Ralph's on Sepulveda Boulevard, about a mile south of the hotel. I had decided that my budget wouldn't allow me the extravagant shopping at Whole Foods® or eating out as a regular habit. Besides, who wanted to sit in a noisy restaurant or bar and wait for average service and receive mediocre food? I decided a better option was to pursue my passion for cooking while developing and perfecting many new dishes.

Ralph's was your typical chain grocery store, middle of the pack in costs and amenities, though in California they sold beer, wine and a selection of spirits for the drinking crowd.

The Purchasing Pattern Begins

In an effort to maximize my buying power and challenge my cooking skills, I decided to start in the meat section, see what was on-sale, and from there select something as the main dish. Then I would choose vegetables, dry goods and dairy products to supplement the meat of the day. It became the beginning of my Tour-de-California. Of course, it required that I purchase more than just the basic cooking selections even for my short-term stays. I had to make decisions on spices, condiments and flavorings as well as parings to the various choices of meat.

I took my first set of basic purchases back to the hotel, loaded the cabinets and turned on the Chopped Series. As it became commonplace for me over the next three-plus years, I spent many hours each week watching the Food Channel to garner new ideas of how to prepare exotic meals that served me well as I expanded my guest list that included travelers from around the world.

For my first meal experience, I purchased a Tri-tip (Santa Maria steak as they call it in Central California) that met my criteria of choice. It was on sale, discounted because it was one day away from the "sale by date," and more importantly it was something I had never cooked in the past. Normally $7.99 a pound, it was on sale for $5.99 and displayed a 50% off sticker. End of life choices must be made quickly and occasionally didn't make it to the dinner table. If it smelled bad, I didn't cook it. The two-and-a-half-pound Tri-tip, normally $19.99, on sale for $14.98 only cost me $7.49. 7.5/20 = 62.5% savings. My first trip to Ralph's was far more successful than I had hoped it to be.

Having never prepared this cut of beef I had assumed it was the same as flank steak. Not so my friends, but close. My next move required some additional research, so I headed to the computer where I completed expeditious treasure hunting. What had I gotten myself in to? I was hungry and about to prepare a cut of meat I had never faced in any of my past culinary endeavors.

Whole pig, yes, but tri-tip had never made it to my cooking station before that special day in EL Segundo.

While searching for recipes, I quickly discovered if I didn't want to ruin this cut of meat, I couldn't cook it like I would a normal steak with just salt, pepper and hot flame on the grill. It was a lean cut of meat with little marbling indicating minimal fat. The internet search did indicate that a tri-tip had good flavor. Success in preparing this cut would require an introduction to developing a marinade into my dossier of skills. I had not initially purchased most of the marinade ingredients, so back I went to Ralph's to secure the following for my Central California Tri-tip marinade:

1. 1/3 cup sugar – I bought a ten-pound bag
2. 1/3 cup Jack Daniels – I used a bit more and had some for additional for tasting
3. 1 teaspoon of ginger – I purchased a whole rhizome of ginger (root), which I peeled and shaved
4. 1 clove crushed/minced garlic – I found a two-pound jar of minced garlic for $4.99

The next step required marinating the steak for a couple of hours, then cooking whole on the grill to a medium rare temperature (130 degrees F). Like most meats, I allowed it to rest for ten minutes before slicing thin against the grain. If I had chosen flank steak, I would have sliced the steak thin after marinating and then cooked to the desired temperature. I discovered that you can either cook the steak whole then slice or slice first and be careful to not overcook the more delicate slices.

A Flank Steak Marinade recipe to produce Steak Fajitas prior to it being sliced thin on the bias:

1. Vegetable oil (many choices here depending on palate and preference)
2. Soy sauce

3. Vinegar
4. Lemon juice
5. Worcestershire sauce (try and say this five times fast)
6. Mustard
7. Minced garlic
8. Black pepper

At least I had the black pepper. It turned out that the 'on sale' piece of meat became an expensive journey for my first meal out of the block.

Slice and Dice – Getting Ahead of the Game

Early in my journey to discover cooking in a hotel room I realized that it would require proper timing and tools to become effective and efficient in the delivery of a fine dining experience. I didn't have enough time each night to prepare an entire meal after working a full day that started at 6:30 A.M. and seldom ended before 5:00 P.M. I learned to make adjustments. I found that planning and preparation was necessary for time management as well as developing good kitchen practices. I created a regular schedule for meal preparation. I realized immediately that the standard kitchen tools provided by the hotel would not suffice for my needs and would requiring another shopping trip that became a long-term investment in some new tools.

My weekly sous chef schedule:

Saturday A.M.	Ralph's grocery store for meats and vegetables and fruit for the week
Saturday P.M.	Create basic menu plan for the week and prepare vegetables
Sunday A.M./P.M.	Prepare dinner and marinate/prep Monday/Tuesday meal
Mon/Tue/Wed P.M.	Complete planned meals and adjust as necessary
Thursday P.M.	Restock vegetables (slice & dice)
Fri/Sat P.M.	Leftovers or complete planned meals

Depending on my local guests for the evening or out of town visitors, the plans and meals changed from individual meals for two to a dinner party of four or five guests. The Residence Inn provided a full breakfast seven days a week and a moderate dinner selection Monday through Thursday. I generally left for work before the breakfast was set up, so I only enjoyed the free breakfast options on Saturdays and Sundays. I rarely ate the dinner provided, although I spent an hour most evenings visiting in the dinner area with other long-term residents and interesting short-term visitors.

My daily meal plans also changed depending on who was working the check-in desk at the hotel. If they hadn't eaten, then I would share my dinner or take requests from the supplies stocked in my refrigerator. My newly developed organization in the kitchen allowed it possible for me to prepare most any meal in forty-five minutes to an hour. I hose different cuts of meats or pasta dishes and tried them out on the evening staff. Many of the new recipes I developed over the three-year period were tested by the hotel staff prior to become a staple in my culinary repertoire.

Eggs-actly – any style, any place, any time

I offer a few pictures of my breakfast creations, although I admit it was a meal I often skipped. Therefore, I did not spend a lot of time building an extensive or creative menu of morning dishes. Everything included eggs. Fried, scrambled, poached not much difference. I added toast and preserves and a side order of whatever meat I have left over from a previous dinner entrée.

I found that a plate of eggs, side of meat and potatoes became a nice and relaxing quick meal any time of day or night. I often prepared eggs late in the evening when the need arose for a quick and nutritional choice. I created the following plates highlighting the egg.

Egg & cheese Omelet w/bacon

Sunny side up w/bacon & fried tortillas

Soft fried eggs on a bed of hash browns

Traditional French toast – 12-hour soak

*Fluffy eggs, polenta,
pork roast and toast*

*Eggs and spinach casserole
in muffin pans*

*Three cheese Jalapeño
Omelet*

*Steak & eggs with fried
potatoes and toast*

Peppers – A Little Knowledge Goes a Long Way

"I'm a pepper, you're a pepper, wouldn't you like to be a Dr. Pepper." Sorry, the topic took me back to a television commercial for Dr. Pepper soda from the early 1970's. There are many kinds of peppers used in cooking and food preparation. I offer a few considerations and information to assist you in choosing peppers based on their intended use rather than just going to the grocery store and randomly grabbing some peppers for your meal. Research studies indicate diets that include spicy peppers are good for a healthy digestive system. I eat jalapenos peppers with many of my meals and almost always when I make a sandwich using leftover meats.

Let's start with the simple bell pepper grown in many gardens for use in salads and as an accompaniment to many meat dishes. Did you know that there is a key difference between male peppers and female peppers? Don't expect the grocery store to separate them for you. The female bell peppers are rounder than the males and have 4 bumps on the bottom. They have more seeds on the inside and are naturally sweeter than the male bell peppers. When planning to use peppers for salad or vegetable trays, you want to choose female peppers. A male bell pepper is taller and thinner than the female pepper and only has 3 bumps on the bottom. Male peppers are not as sweet as female peppers however, they hold up better in heat and therefore are better for cooking. These are perfect for stews, dips, and general-purpose cooking. If you are going to make stuffed peppers, I recommend you use male peppers with three bumps on the bottom the larger, even though the shorter, rounder female peppers with the more solid base appear more esthetically correct and less likely to fall over.

Does color matter when choosing bell peppers? Yes, a bit. A red bell pepper is simply a ripened green bell pepper, though there is a variety called Permagreen that remain green when ripe. The green peppers are less sweet and slightly more bitter than yellow, orange or red peppers. The red pepper is the sweetest. Don't forget that a female pepper is sweeter than the male pepper.

Get your "red hots" Peppers – "Proceed with Caution"

Although many people don't like "heat" in their foods, research has proven that eating hot peppers has several health benefits, which I have below. I caution the reader that when one embarks on the introduction of 'heat' in the kitchen, please do it cautiously and gradually. One's palate can become used to the enhanced temperature and the varying tastes of spicy peppers over time. Many cultures start their children at very young ages. Introducing too much heat too fast can be dangerous and your casual guests may never return. If not introduced in moderation too much heat will produce a great burning sensation on your lips, mouth, tongue and throat. It can cause severe heartburn resulting in spasms of the diaphragm, creating uncontrollable hiccups. Making matters worse, when the extreme and intense heat of the peppers completes its path through your alimentary canal, you will once again experience the burn of the pepper. "What goes in, must come out."
Quoting from PepperHEAD® dated June 22, 2018

"The documented health benefits from hot peppers continue to grow at a break-neck speed, similar to the increasing popularity of consuming hot foods in various forms." The heat and health benefits come from a chemical called capsaicin. If all I have read recently on the health benefits of hot peppers is true, I'll need to create a new quote for the growing health-conscious public; something like: "Hot Tamales Today, Healthy Body Tomorrow"

Historically, spicy additions to food helped prevent spoilage in warm climates before the invention of refrigeration. Capsaicin's anti-microbial properties inhibit as much as 75% of bacteria growth. People from cultures who lived and survived due to the use of various spices passed down to the next of kin spicy recipes and taste buds that desired extra zing in their food.

Adding hot peppers, hot sauces and hot powders to food continues to protect us from food poisoning even though we now refrigerate food. To maximize these health benefits, eating the hottest pepper would magnify these effects."

10 Amazing Benefits to Eating Hot Peppers (Scientifically Proven)

1. Benefits to the Digestive Track,
2. Promotes a Healthy Heart,
3. Mitigates Migraines,
4. Relieves Joint Pain,
5. Improves Metabolism (Promotes Weight Loss),
6. Quells Psoriasis,
7. Reduces Cancer Risk,
8. Fights the Flu, Colds and Fungal Infections,
9. Prevents Bad Breath,
10. Prevents Allergies.

From PepperHEAD® dated June 22, 2018

So, how hot is hot? Yes, we must throw caution to the wind. One needs to know before proceeding forward that Capsaicin is the chemical responsible for the "heat" level of different varieties of peppers and is defined as Scoville Heat Units (SHU). Begin small and work your way down the chart and always advise your dinner guests when you intend to introduce "heat" in your offerings. As in any spice, you can always add more and never subtract once you have saturated your dish.

A popular pepper used in many Mexican/Hispanic dishes and often stuffed in the poblano pepper, readily available in most grocery stores. Many people consider the poblano as a mild pepper; however growing conditions can create a wide range of heat. A wet and moderate growing season will produce peppers with less heat index because of the more favorable growing conditions. When the growing season is hot and little water is available, the plant tends to protect itself by producing greater levels of Capsaicin to protect it from natural predators.

The SHU of the Poblano pepper is 1,500 and would take approximately 1,500 cups of water diluted into it to no longer feel any burning sensation in your mouth.

I have grown my own peppers for a number of years in the small garden I plant. I offer one caution here. If you are growing your own hot peppers, you must be careful how close your peppers grow together because they can cross pollinate and what you assume to be a mild pepper can in fact produce an almost toxic heat level. Be careful with the growing process and handle the plants and fruit wearing gloves. Never work with peppers and then uses your hand to wipe the sweat from your eyes; it will feel as if you had pepper spray in your eyes.

Peppers I have cultivated and used in my cooking include:

1. Bell: green, red, yellow, orange
2. Banana
3. Cherry
4. Anaheim
5. Poblano
6. Scotch bonnets
7. Cayenne
8. Thai
9. Jalapeno
10. Habanero
11. Ghost

Scoville Heat Unit (SHU)	Variety of Peppers
1,000,000	Ghost pepper
800,000 – 3,200,000	Pepper X, Carolina Reaper, Dragon's Breath, Naga Morich
350,000 – 800,000	Red Savina pepper, Chocolate Habanero
100,000 – 350,000	Habanero, Scotch Bonnet
10,000 – 100,000	Malagueta pepper, Cayenne pepper
1,000 – 10,000	Guajillo pepper, Jalapeno pepper
100 – 1,000	Banana pepper, Cubanelle
0 – 100	Bell pepper, Pimento

Chart Depicting Scoville Heat Unit and associated Peppers credit Wikipedia® 1/22/2019

As my pepper plants grew and matured, I selected a few of the peppers from each variety to use in some dishes and also took time to evaluate the SCU index in my cooking. When I harvested my peppers at the end of the growing season, I prepared them for storage and future use. The bell peppers were always washed, tops cut off, seeds removed, parboiled and frozen for storage and use throughout the winter and spring. If the peppers were in good shape, I would leave them whole and made stuffed peppers, if not, I cleaned, sliced the peppers then froze them.

When it came to storing the hot peppers, I used two methods: 1) Cleaned and freeze-dried and, 2) Dry storage - uprooted the entire plant and hung them upside-down in my basement where they dried over the winter for future use. In the following spring I pulled the dried peppers off of the plants, ground them and put stored them sealed jars and Ziploc® bags. It was important to have carefully sealed the storage containers to ensure no moisture remained that would allow the peppers and seeds to grow mold and rot. Unlike many varieties of cheese, mold on peppers is never a good thing.

One early spring season, my youngest granddaughter, McKenzie, four-years-old at the time, was visiting me and wanted to help me plant my seeds to grow the seedlings and later transplant to the garden. I told her to be careful around the plants and showed her how to put a depression in the starter pots, add a couple of seeds, cover them with dirt and mist water onto each pot. I also told her to be extremely careful and to not wipe her face or put her fingers in her mouth. I let her plant some herbs, beans and tomatoes. Suddenly she started screaming and crying. She had gotten into my jalapeño pepper seeds and put her fingers in her mouth. The pain and crying only lasted a few minutes; however, the grief I received for allowing her to touch the peppers lasted for a long time.

Riding the Gravy Train – Gravy by Any Other Name is still a Sauce

Sauces are liquids of various thicknesses that are flavored or seasoned to enhance the flavor of food. Sauces can be sweet, sour, spicy, or savory and may be added to the food to become part of a main dish or used as an accompaniment to the food being prepared. They add a variety of features to foods, such as complementing or enhancing flavors, adding an attractive appearance, and/or providing additional texture.

Initially perfected by the French, all sauces are now universally categorized into one of seven groups of sauces that serve as base sauces or foundations for other sauces known as *secondary sauces*. The primary sauces are known as *Grand Sauces* or *Mother Sauces*.

The following are the categories of the Mother Sauces of French cooking from which all other sauces are prepared:

1. White Sauces - such as Béchamel Sauce
2. Brown Sauces (such as Madeira Sauce)
3. Tomato Sauces or Red Sauces (such as Tomato Puree)
4. Egg Yolk and Butter Sauces (such as Hollandaise Sauce)
5. Egg Yolk and Oil Sauces (such as Mayonnaise)
6. Oil and Vinegar Sauces (such as Salad Dressing)
7. Flavored Butter Sauces (such as Bruere Blanc Sauce)

I heard many terms being used for simple processes like sauces. I learned that my journey to become a self-made chef wasn't going to be as simple as first imagined. If I was to become a successful chef it required I learn the terms and the different means of doing even simple sauces.

Then I learned there were yet Other Common Sauce Terms:

1. Reduction Sauce
2. Secondary Sauce
3. Small Sauce
4. Finishing Sauce
5. Pan Sauce

Yes … gravy is a sauce, just in case you thought I missed one You will never hear a true chef use the word gravy; too common for a five-star kitchen. Merriam-Webster tells us that gravy is a sauce made from the thickened and seasoned juices of cooked meat. Much like the Bubba Gump quotes, there are many kinds of shrimp to consider. When someone mentions gravy with a meal it can mean many different things to many people. Clarity is critical in meeting the diner's expectation.

1. Dressing
2. Sauce
3. Condiment
4. Relish
5. Seasoning
6. Fixing(s)
7. Garnish
8. Topping
9. Dip
10. Marinade

I expect by now your brain is swimming in the sauce(s). Never fear it's not that difficult to manage. I seldom use more than one or two simple sauces for most of my meals, except when celebrities come for dinner and expect something fabulous from the kitchen. My solution then is to go to YouTube® for assistance.

Many Nights in Front of the Television – I schooled myself one meal at a time

I studied the art and the language of cooking while I binge-watched the Food Channel. The hosts and judges used fancy terms for simple sauces one must use when performing on television like: Remoulade Sauce, Béarnaise Sauce, Peppercorn Sauce, Mushroom Sauce, Cheese Sauces, and Chimichurri. It didn't stop there; they also shared an entire genre of Wine Reduction Sauces (one is likely to get sauced with these for sure). I have read several books on Julia Child and watched the movie *Julie and Julia* where a young chef decided to recreate every recipe in Julia Child's book. Julia was definitely drawn to the sauces, especially sipping of the wine as she prepared her meals and accompanying sauces. Now, that's my kind of entertaining cooking show and she was extremely entertaining.

If that isn't enough to impress the novice while enlightening the pallet along the way, there are five mother Sauces:

1. Béchamel Sauce
2. Velouté Sauce
3. Espagnole Sauce
4. Hollandaise Sauce
5. Classic Tomato Sauce

Summarizing my additional research, I could not find that any single sauce has been deemed, "The Mother of All Sauces" though my grandmother made one heck of a sausage sauce she poured all over fresh baked buttermilk biscuits. She led a simple life and just called it gravy.

BTW, a question comes to mind, "Why do we need a Roux just to thicken a sauce and when do we need to use clarified butter instead of just regular butter"? The experts say it is because clarified butter has twenty percent less water than typical butter, so does that make it special? Do you think the cow would know the difference? And, please don't tell me you think it's alright to cook with margarine like Chiffon®, because "It's not nice to fool Mother Nature "or "You think it's butter but it's not." Do you know when to cook with salted verses unsalted butter?

And while we are at it, don't confuse sauces with dressings either, that would be a faux pas; French for an embarrassing or tactless act or remark in a social situation. And by the way, dressings aren't just used as a liquid-based preparation to pour on top of a salad to make it edible. Perhaps we'll cover those differences later, however only if you ask nicely.

Bringing Southeastern Cooking (Soul Food) to the West Coast

There is an extensive list of Southern Foods and depending on how far East, South or towards the Midwest one lives, tradition and availability of ingredients generally dictates the dinner menu. In the early days of emigration from Europe and beyond to the United States different cultures and foods settled in different sections of the country. I have enjoyed many a dish from the Louisiana Bayou that came from the French colonization of the area and have cooked a lot of gumbo. However, that type of regional fare was not a staple in my repertoire as a child growing up. Until we moved in a community on the Severn River in Severna Park, Maryland where I developed a taste for fish and crabs, most of my dining experience had come from the Eastern North Carolina area plus my mother's deep Italian roots. Most of it came directly from the kitchen of my grandmother, Lillian Pearson. Our grandfather Harvey was a self-taught finish carpenter by trade and built their house at 1902 Nast Street N. in Wilson, North Carolina. The house granddaddy built was a one-story, two-bedroom home with only one bathroom where they raised five kids. In the day, life was far simpler than today's giant mansions with more bathrooms than bedrooms.

Coming from a poor family where my parents and grandparents lived and the period of history known as the Great Depression, our food selections were limited to a simple and standard palate of tastes. The following entrees and inexpensive side dishes were always available in Grandmother Pearson's kitchen. There was always plenty to eat, just not the expensive choices.

Pork sausage & buttermilk biscuits w/molasses (left out on the stove for days)	Hash brown potatoes Beef stew Pork BBQ Brunswick stew

Fried chicken

Boiled potatoes

Mashed potatoes & gravy

Country ham

Fried baloney

Homemade preserves &
 lots of apple butter

Pork rinds

Hominy

Grits

Dick's Red hotdogs
 (Saturday treat)

Parker's Pork BBQ
 (Holidays with the
 Pearson Clan)

Pecan pie (from the trees
 in the backyard)

Collard greens

Spinach

Corn

Peas

Green beans

Kale

Pancakes & bacon

Cobblers; peach, apple,
 cherry

Turkey
 (Thanksgiving only)

Ham (mainly
 Christmas time)

I'm pretty sure that everything was either cooked with or in lard at Grandmother Pearson's house. There was always a ten-pound tub of lard stashed between the refrigerator and the stove. When we were real young (1950's), the refrigerator was of the old style: wooden frame, with tin inserts, a drip pan and a large box for block ice from the time that predated electricity in most houses. This appliance did not have an electrical plug or ice maker. It required going to the local ice house for large blocks of ice that would last four or five days at a time.

Holidays – The Seasons to Share food and love with family and friends

We celebrated the traditional holidays when most people have a few days off at the same time which allowed for travel to and from one's home to another's. This was a tradition I remember as a kid when we rode in the back of Dad's 1956 Plymouth sedan. We drove from Maryland to Grandmother's house on West Nash Street every Thanksgiving, Christmas and Easter. Every year the Harvey Pearson clan gathered at grandmothers where us grandchildren would all sleep on the living room floor on pallets (thin blankets) my grandmother had made over the years. Dad had two sisters and two brothers and there were thirteen of us cousins. There were a lot of people sleeping in that 1,000 square foot, one-story house.

Every Thanksgiving we recreated the ritual where our dads would supervise the cousins as we picked up all the fallen pecans from granddaddy's three large pecan trees. We would gather thousands of pecans. Our fathers would climb high in the tree and shake the long limbs until all of the pecans had fallen. We would fill large five-gallon wash tubs with pecans ever year. Years later it would be determined that this game was actually child-labor because we were paid nothing for our efforts. Uncle Curtis Burton Pearson would sit on the full tub of pecans and then offer us a penny for each additional pecan we found. Hunt and find as we may, I don't remember Uncle Curtis ever paying anybody even one red cent, not even his own kids: Gene-Ann, Betsy and Robert. He did however give me a coronet when I was in the 6th grade so I could learn to play music and join both the concert and marching bands through high school.

Southern Fried Cooking –
A family tradition of 'grease and greens'

My mom's family hails from Italy via emigration to Glastonbury, Connecticut and my dad's mainly from England and his family had settled in Wilson, North Carolina. Since the price of New England seafood was out as an option for us, we ate a lot of good old Southern cuisine growing up. Location plus the significant difference in cost of these food options led us to fried foods and lots of greens; collards, kale, spinach, mustard greens, beet greens and cabbage.

If you are traveling through Eastern North Carolina on or near Interstate I-95, I recommend you stop and eat at Parkers BBQ, located at 2514 US-301, Wilson, NC 27893. The menu provides for both Carolina Pork BBQ and deep-fried chicken. "Where's the beef"? There isn't any at Parkers. Each of the chicken fryers contain at least ten gallons of hot cooking oil. Make sure you order Brunswick stew, you won't be disappointed. I also suggest that you get the platter because you don't want to miss out on a combination of Brunswick Stew, Boiled Potatoes, Cole Slaw and Corn Sticks. Eat the corn sticks while they are hot though, as they aren't worth saving for another day. Day-old corn sticks will have hardened like a hockey puck.

During my research of North Carolina eateries, I discovered the work of the well-known television reporter/author, Scott Mason of WRAL television in Raleigh, North Carolina. He published a delicious and informative book titled, *TAR HEEL TRVELER EATS: FOOD JOURNEY'S ACROSS NORTH CAROLINA*. I enjoyed following his own travels in the search for food and people as I read the book and a discovered that a few of his selections are my favorites from my childhood in Wilson, North Carolina; Dicks Hotdog Stand on my grandmothers' street; West Nash and Parker's Barbeque. Scott has more than 100 journalism awards including twenty regional Emmys and three National Edward R. Murrow awards.

His book describes his personal journey across the state where he describes the eatery, the history of the location and the food they prepare.

Just Can't Live without Fried Foods

I mentioned my Food Intake Modification Plan (FIMP) and the fact that during my personal journey I lost over fifty pounds through a lean cooking discipline. I must admit though that I have prepared and will always enjoy fried foods. I continue to do this today and on occasion still fry the following menu items, though not as often and in limited quantities.

Inventory of my favorite Fried Foods:

Chicken
Chicken gizzards
Chicken liver
Chicken skin
Pork rinds
French fries
Fried dough
Stuffed mushrooms
Calamari
Fish (many varieties)
Okra
Cheeseburgers
Corn dogs
Green beans
Scallops
Clams
Mussels
Salmon cakes
Shrimp
Crawdads
Prawns
Maryland crab cakes
Crab puffs
Crab balls

Burritos
Enchiladas
Chilies Relleno
Taquitos
Spring rolls
Pot stickers
Grits
Tempura
Egg rolls
Wontons
Hush puppies
Sweet potatoes
Donuts
Cronuts
Noodles

Unplanned West Coast Culinary Tour

The first two recipes I chose to share with my newfound west coast friends in EL Segundo, California were North Carolina pork barbeque (BBQ) and Southern Fried Chicken. Fried chicken to done properly requires lots of oil, a high temperature and a deep fryer (when possible). Carolina pork BBQ requires a large covered pan and an oven temperature set to 200 – 225 F degrees. Fried chicken is considered a quick-cook meal where pork must be slow cooked or smoked for barbeque dishes to be best prepared. Everyone can purchase Kentucky Fried Chicken (KFC®) and coleslaw, however few people where I was stationed knew how to deep fry well-seasoned and produce moist crispy fried chicken while duplicating The Colonel's famous recipes.

For the first three months preparing meals for myself and the evening desk staff, the fare consisted mainly of the basic east coast dishes that I had been preparing many years for my family. When I would swing through the lobby after working all day the first greeting was, "Hey Mr. Pearson, what are you cooking tonight"? They knew if I was cooking, there was always enough to share and they wouldn't have to fend for themselves and settle for carry-out options. It became a regular pastime and I generally cooked for the guest services team three or four times a week.

Chez Eric Restaurant, El Segundo, California
My Residence Inn kitchen
where food and conversation flowed freely

From Fried Chicken to Pulled Port Barbeque – Southern Cooking at Its Best

As I began feeding the hotel management team and front desk staff, I had chosen to offer my family favorites from the Southeast of the United States. I had decided that those were safe meals I had prepared hundreds of times before and despite the limited cooking facilities in my hotel room, I was able to provide a quality meal at a reasonable expense to me. I never charged the staff or my guests to share my preparations. They were always my guests when it came to sharing a meal and in exchange, I gained friendships and lengthy conversations.

I began my West Coast journey through cooking with pulled pork barbeque (BBQ). Since I knew that everyone was aware of how to fry chicken one way or another that was my second option. Properly preparing pork entrees required that I purchase a large roasting pan because most pork shoulders ranged between seven to ten pounds. I wasn't ready yet to expand my cooking vessels to include a deep fryer and a large crock pot (slow cooker) though they were soon to become a staple asset in my multi-purpose kitchen/bedroom/living room.

Using the roaster allowed me to prepare the pork the evening before, dress and marinates it and then put it in my preheated oven at 225 degrees to cook all day while I was at work. The later addition of two crock pot slow cookers made it easier to vary the cooking time and to maintain the meat on warm after the cooking period was complete. Meals cooked and simmered while I was at work. I would often run back to the room at lunchtime to check on the progress. I always provided coleslaw, boiled potatoes, sweet yellow corn and breadsticks when I served pork BBQ.

After successfully preparing and sharing pork BBQ to rave reviews, the next move was to create a real Southern Fried Chicken dinner. That process required a choice of a large round deep-frying pan, a large cast iron skillet, or a professionally manufactured deep fryer. My grandmother only used large cast iron skillets. Over the period of the first six months in California I progressed from the frying pan, to an iron skillet and eventually to a deep fryer. To become successful the home-grown chef must start the frying process with the oil of choice between 350 to 375 degrees. The addition of the chicken into the hot oil quickly dropped the temperature of the oil and it became important to maintain a temperature close to 325 degrees during the frying period. It generally took twelve to fifteen minutes to completely deep fry the larger pieces of chicken. I turned the chicken frequently and cooked it until the pieces were crispy and golden brown. The chicken pieces cooked at different rates. Legs and thighs took longer than breasts and wings. I did not want to serve chicken that was uncooked and pink or bloody around the joints, so I cut into it to check doneness. I also used a thermometer, looking for 165 degrees.

I have always preferred extra crispy chicken and often ate the skin and save the white meat to make chicken salad instead of eating it fresh from the fryer. To ensure crispy chicken I double or even triple dipped the chicken pieces. Here is one method I used where I triple dipped my chicken pieces before deep frying:

1. In a medium size bowl mix 3 cups of flour, 1 tablespoon garlic salt, 1 tablespoon black pepper, ½ teaspoon paprika, and 1 tablespoon of poultry seasoning.

2. In a separate bowl stir 1/3 cup flour, salt, ¼ teaspoon pepper, three egg yolks, and ½ cup of beer. If batter is too thick, thin with additional beer. Drink excess beer.

3. Heat the oil in a deep-fryer to 350 degrees F (175 degrees C).

4. Moisten each piece of chicken with a little water, and then dip in the dry mix. Shake off excess and dip in the wet mix, then dip in the dry mix once more.

5. Using metal tongs carefully place the chicken pieces in the hot oil. Fry for 15 to 18 minutes, or until well browned. Smaller pieces will be done sooner. Large pieces may take longer. Remove and drain on paper towels before serving.

6. Do not crowd the frying pan or the temperature will drop significantly. Allow oil to come up in temperature before adding each new batch of chicken

7. Cook same size pieces together for an even result.

Adapted from Allrecipes January, 2019

I decided to run with the odds and having secured positive impressions of my kitchen skills at the very beginning of this culinary journey, I pursued the basic entrees and at first comfortably offered several varieties of food from the South to:

1. The management team,
2. the front desk staff,
3. the long-term selected short-term residents, and
4. anyone who inspired me with their genre of conversation.

It became a three-year study of food and people at The Residence Inn. In my past, I had produced a lot of open campfire meals growing up in the Boy Scouts of America (BSA), but that wasn't going to cut it if I was to survive in Southern California for more than a minute.

I realized pretty quickly that a hotel studio does not come well equipped to prepare more than the basic meals. You get a couple of thin clad pots and pans with ill-fitting lids, a set four dishes, two medium size serving bowls, four forks, knives and spoons, one or two ladles, one sharp and two dull knives and a small paring knife.

Over the period of the first six months at The Residence Inn between the kindness of the hotel manager and her senior staff and my own purchases I accumulated the following appliances and cooking implements. These were stored by the hotel when I checked out every three to six weeks when I returned home to Baltimore or other occasional travel requirements for my employer. Upon my arrival back at the hotel after each trip, all of my storage was always back in my room ready for the next group meal preparation.

Tools of the Trade stored by The Residence Inn during my trips back home:

Crockpots (2)	Deep fryer (1)	Large ironclad pot (2)
Rice steamer (1)	Baking pan (3)	Tabletop oven
Griddle (1)	Pizza pan (2)	Large serving bowls (3)
Aluminum foil	Parchment paper	Flour, potatoes, grits, onions, sugar …
Cast iron skillet	Double broiler (1)	Waffle iron (1)
Cheese grater	Quality set of knives	Cooking utensils (various)

And a large box of assorted spices from the Orient

It was a continual negotiation as to who was responsible for purchasing new pieces of the inventory to compliment the kitchen set. It generally came down that I purchased the items as they didn't need them. However, when I was away other residents would ask to borrow them: crockpot, steamer, deep fryer, rice cooker. On occasion I would return and discover that some of my tools were missing from storage, as they had been loaned out to other residents who fancied themselves as chefs. At the conclusion of my three-year experience in El Segundo, California and hotel living, I left all of my cooking vessels and utensils with the Residence Inn to be loaned to other long-term guests.

My early Cooking Vessels in El Segundo Studio at The Residence Inn 2011 – 2014

Two crockpots – cook while you work and feed six to ten at once

*Preparing for storage of
my supplies when I went home*

When I packed up everything for my short trips home to Maryland, for a couple of days, I had to pack everything in my hotel room. The Residence Inn staff stored all of my cooking supplies plus they stored all of my clothes, camping supplies, daily cooking implements and dry goods. This allowed me to fly back and forth across the country with only one small carry-on and my computer bag. I would pack and store as much as I could and the cleaning staff took home any extra perishables, I had left in the refrigerator for them. Often, I stocked the fridge the day before leaving as my gift for the excellent service.

The regular routine I kept allowed for me to ensure there was always an abundance of supplies left in the fridge. It also meant if I was short some items for my cooking or in need of an extra cooking pot, there was always someone willing to provide it for my use.

We became family, helping each other in times of need and loaded with conversation.

It's a Dog's World After All – Riggs and Rye

I worked with several engineers who were semi-permanently stationed in El Segundo, California and assigned to the projects I was worked on. One young engineer needed to return to Baltimore shortly after being transferred to California for her two-year assignment. She had recently driven across country with her mother and her two dogs to settle in.

We had spoken about our pets during one of the dinners I had prepared for our young engineers. I shared that I had several dogs and cats back home and it was lonely being in a studio by myself all the time. She asked if I might be willing to keep her two dogs while she returned to Baltimore, since her new landlord was not willing to take care of them in her absence.

It had become a time for me to step up or step out. An opportunity to have company was intriguing however the responsibility of caring for two animals I did not know was concerning. It also required that I negotiate with the hotel to allow the dogs in the room for two weeks. I met Riggs and Rye and we spent one day getting to know each other. It went well so I said I would do it. Twice a day we walked the grounds, picked up their deposits and returned to our tiny room.

They were good dogs and a pleasure to have as guests. I did have to make a decision about informing the hotel staff about the dogs and to negotiate the $75 per pet residence fee and the $250 required cleaning fee once they left. I decided to let the staff make the first move. I knew it was impossible to hide them and everybody saw me walking them twice a day and as I often tossed them tennis balls on the basketball court. Funny thing, not one of the staff ever mentioned the dogs or the fees. It was like we all knew the situation and it was our little secret, everybody's little secret. I'm sure if we had ever had the discussion, I would not have been charged the fees. We were family, some things go unnoticed or spoken about.

I did feel guilty about not openly addressing the dogs on site, and to relieve my anxiety, I made extra meals and fed the staff daily instead of only two to three times a week. Is it a bribe when you provide something to someone and sort of get something in return when there was never a conversation, not a wink or smile, no mention of "quid pro quo"?

Gone to the dogs: Riggs and Rye – my guests for two weeks

Mari Estrada – It's good to get to know your hotel manager

Because I was a long-term resident, I decided at the beginning that I would only request my room be cleaned and the linins changed once a week. I felt it wasn't necessary to exercise the staff daily, it saved time, energy and water; always a good habit to adopt. The ladies who cleaned the rooms every day always asked if I needed anything and if I wanted spare towels, cooking utensils or paper supplies. The few times I said I needed something; the items appeared in my room while I was still at work.

Over those three years I lived at The Residence Inn I experienced many changes in the staff and of course residents. Long-term residents came and went. Staff members grew in experiences and moved on to greater opportunities. My first contact and who quickly became a friend Mari, was promoted from Director of Marketing and Corporate Contracts to the position as Hotel Manager after I had been a resident the first year. She kept a cadre of excellent employees around her who ensured a quality and family atmosphere was provided day in and day out. They maintained over 95% occupancy rate during my stay with the Residence Inn family from 2011 through 2014.

Mari Estrada – Residence Inn Manager
and gift prints they gave me when I retired

When I was about to complete my last week of the three-year assignment in EL Segundo, Mari held a surprise going away party in my honor. All of the hotel staff was there. That included: the management team, the desk services folks, the maintenance team and all of the wonderful women who cleaned the rooms, the dining area and the lobby; seven days a week, three-hundred-sixty-five days a year. They not only baked me a cake, they gave me two prints of chefs to celebrate my cooking journey. That was a tough day for me as I was leaving my large family and facing retirement. Tears flowed as we laughed about all the interesting people who had crossed our paths during the previous three years together. I had brought basic Southern Fried cooking from my roots to Southern California where Mexican and Hispanic foods reigned as King, and I took back with me their culture. We had shared great recipes featuring family tradition and combined several very different cultures through our numerous culinary exchanges.

How to Survive Round Three on Chopped – Dessert

Desserts, pastries and baking in general are far more difficult than preparing appetizers, main dishes and ala carte vegetables. When preparing most dishes, the chef has several opportunities to taste and add seasoning to the meal. When baking, there is only one chance to get it correct. Combining the ingredients happens in steps, however once the dish is prepared there is no going back to add additional seasonings or ingredients. I avoided deserts and pastries for that reason as well as I had embarked on my lean cooking adventure. I knew that my will power was never strong enough to stop after eating only one or two donuts much less # 13 of a baker's dozen.

When I began my cult-like pursuit of The Food Channel and Chopped, I became aware that there were multiple steps working with mystery ingredients necessary to win the competition and the $10,000 prize. One had to survive these three stages during the competition to avoid being chopped: appetizer, main dish and dessert. I was confident I could make it through the appetizer round and the key point was to make sure that you didn't produce a main dish or large quantity. I had been creating and serving main dishes for years, so other that the time restraint I felt comfortable I could make it through round two.

Round three and dessert, now that would be a different story all together. I had little to no experience with pastries and honestly wasn't sure I could even create a potential solution if I even made it to this final round. Until I watched several episodes of *Chopped*, I had not known what an anti-griddle was, did not know how to use the ice-cream maker, had no clue why to balancing sweet and savory was necessary, and I was never any good at exact measures; all of which are critical in dessert preparation. Somehow though I was going to have to learn some skills in the unlikely chance I would get called to appear on the show.

Donuts to Croissants to Cronuts – A sticky situation not recommended for the amateur

I loved to make homemade biscuits and fresh bread from scratch, loading them with real butter and homemade jams. Twice a year using four bread makers, I had made fifty to sixty pizza doughs for my Leadership Training Program (LTP) weekend summits. Occasional I would create fresh baked lattice topped pies for holiday dinners. I had always thought the recipes and level of difficulty for biscuits, bread and pizza dough required moderate culinary skills. However, I avoided with a passion the more demanding and precise requirements of desserts. I could hide no longer; it was time I moved on and faced my greatest fears.

I practiced the steps and expanded my culinary vocabulary while I increased my limited skills as a faux pastry chef. I began teaching myself how to make donuts, croissants and the greatest challenge, cronuts.

"Warning: Investment required"

*As the saying goes,
"If you can't do the time, don't do the crime."*

Time to prep properly and cook

Donuts -	two to two and a half hours
Croissants -	four to four and a half hours
Cronuts -	five to six hours to two days

Donuts

Donuts did not appear to be a difficult endeavor other than being a multiple step process and management of the critical rising and resting times necessary to allow the yeast and sugar to do their thing, otherwise you will produce flat donuts. It was a sticky operation on my first attempt, and second and third. Practice makes possible, seldom perfect. I made sure that the yeast and sugar combination was at the proper temperature to facilitate the optimal rise of the dough. This phase required a two-step process of rising and resting, punching the donuts and holes and then cooking in a pan of hot oil maintained at 350 degrees. The first rise consumed about an hour and a half where the dough doubled in size. I placed it in a warm corner of the kitchen covered with waxed paper to ensure it rose properly. After punching the donuts and holes, the second rise took approximately forty minutes.

When frying donuts, I found it was similar to chicken. It was important the avoid putting too much product in the fryer at the same time because a significant drop in temperature would have caused the delicate donuts to soak up excess oil and become doughy. After frying one pan of donuts, flipping them over to ensure even cooking on both sides, I let the oil temperature rise back to 350 degrees before inserting the next set. I watched the donuts closely in the fryer as it would have been easy to go from near-perfection to burnt beyond crisp in a matter of seconds.

I placed the hot donuts on parchment paper to cool and topped them with my favorite confectionary sugar glaze, no sprinkles. Sampling during this final step was a requirement to maintain Quality Control (QC). Careful, I burnt my lip and the roof of my mouth in my haste to test the end product.

Croissants as the French would say, Voila
Much to my displeasure I learned that a croissant was not just a difficult variation of bread, rolls or biscuits because it required a lot more effort to produce a bakeable product. As we learned from our studies of Hamlet, I am reminded of the quote "Alas poor Yorick" and its reference to the brevity of life. I decided I had to pursue what I had begun before it was too late in life to pursue what appeared to be the impossible task. This became one effort that was quite time consuming. The best part though is it required lots of butter. Who doesn't love butter?

According to my research through the annals of Wikipedia, "A croissant is a buttery, flaky, viennoiserie pastry of Austrian origin, named for its historical crescent shape. Croissants and other viennoiserie are made of layered yeast-leavened dough."

The Breathing of Life into Croissants – An Engineers Version of a not so simple process

1. Combine yeast, warm water, and 1 teaspoon sugar. Allow to stand until creamy and frothy.

2. Measure flour into a mixing bowl. Dissolve 2 teaspoons sugar and salt in warm milk. Blend into flour along with yeast and oil. Mix well; knead until smooth. Cover, and let rise until over triple in volume, about 3 hours. Deflate gently, and let rise again until doubled, about another 3 hours. Deflate and chill 20 minutes.

3. Massage butter until pliable, but not soft and oily. Pat dough into a 14x8-inch rectangle. Smear butter over top two thirds, leaving 1/4-inch margin all around. Fold unbuttered third over middle third, and buttered top third down over that. Turn 90 degrees, so that folds are to left and right. Roll out to a 14x6-inch rectangle. Fold in three again. Sprinkle lightly with flour, and put dough in a plastic bag. Refrigerate 2 hours. Unwrap, sprinkle with flour, and deflate gently. Roll to a 14x6-inch rectangle, and fold again. Turn 90 degrees, and repeat. Wrap, and chill 2 hours.

4. To shape, roll dough out to a 20x5-inch rectangle. Cut in half crosswise, and chill half while shaping the other half. Roll out to a 15 x 5-inch rectangle. Cut into three 5 x 5-inch squares. Cut each square in half diagonally. Roll each triangle lightly to elongate the point, and make it 7 inches long. Grab the other 2 points, and stretch them out slightly as you roll it up. Place on a baking sheet, curving slightly. Let shaped croissants rise until puffy and light. In a small bowl, beat together egg and 1 tablespoon water. Glaze croissants with egg wash.

5. Bake in a preheated 475 degrees F (245 degrees C) oven for 12 to 15 minutes.

Though it took quite an effort and though I managed to spread butter and flour dust all over every surface in my hotel room, I accomplished the challenge and created a delicious mound of butter disguised as flaky bread that looked more like an Atlantic Welk Sea shell from the ocean than a traditional croissant. Despite the amount of butter verses flour ratio, one always adds more butter to a warm croissant when eating in addition to often adding a favorite jam. I dare say you won't find these recipes on any diet known to man or woman.

Cronut – The New York Invention

A croissant donut without the hole in the middle is the best way I can explain what a cronut is. I quired, "Is this even possible to reproduce"? Either way, I was committed to try. Much to my chagrin (no, not a bruised shin) I had no idea that the step up to making cronuts was going to be such a great challenge. Since it was, I decided to honor the process with its own chapter rather than include with donuts and croissants as originally planned. It was like, "separating the wheat from the chaff" kind of a move.

I also learned that only a fool who had recently experienced moderate success making homemade donuts and shortly thereafter created a bevy of croissants would dare venture further into the baking side of the kitchen and attempt to duplicate the latest craze out of New York City.

By May of 2013, I was eighteen months into my three-year assignment out West. By then I had learned all of the basics of cooking and it seemed appropriate to accept the personal challenge of making cronuts. Cronuts had just become the rage of the East and I wanted to see what all the excitement was about. Nobody in El Segundo at the hotel or my peers at work had even heard of cronuts. That meant (to me at least) that I was about to introduce a new delicacy West of the Mississippi, no matter how my creation came out.

A Cronut is a croissant-doughnut pastry invented by New York City pastry chef Dominique Ansel of Dominique Ansel Bakery in New York City; self-proclaimed as the center of the universe. The pastry resembles a doughnut and is made from croissant-like dough which is filled with flavored cream and fried in grapeseed oillicacy. I was about to embark on a mission and if successful, introduce cronuts to Los Angeles County, California.

I had thought the process to make croissants was difficult because it required several steps and waiting periods. In order to make cronuts one was required to start as if making donuts, then take that raised dough and begin the process of making croissants only to veer in a different direction with additional steps necessary to create the now famous cronut. I spent an entire evening following the detailed directions and found myself 'rising' at 4:00 a.m. to complete the process. I still had to fry the cronuts before transporting them to work at 6:30 a.m. Yes, I followed the short version, not the three-day process.

The cronuts were well received I think only because engineers would eat anything given to them for free and systems engineers in particular roam the building in search of day-old donuts every morning. They were not interested in the story of cronuts, how I created them, nor how much difficulty I had overcome to prepare their morning tasting. They seemed to only care that they were fresh, tasted good and were free.

I only wish I had conducted more research and gained some expert advice before I began this quest; such as the following posted in 2016, three years after my pastry experience.

"In anticipation of his upcoming cookbook, last week Dominique Ansel bestowed upon us a make-at-home version of his famous Cronut. The croissant-doughnut hybrid recipe takes three days to make, requires a slew of special equipment, and only produces about eight precious pastries. Obviously, I had to try it out."

Credit: Ariel Knutson' News & Culture Editor,
Los Angeles 2016

Nevertheless, I proceeded and experienced relatively decent success. I claimed a six on a scale of 0 to 10 for the art of building and baking my first and only attempt at cronuts. There is not enough time left in my life to spend three days just to create six to eight delectable cronuts. Next time I have the urge to prepare cronuts I'll find a talented baker and pay the eight to ten dollars required to acquire one.

Cronut Recipe Borrowed from Allspices Recipes – this is the one I recreated in my kitchen in 2013.

Prep and cooking time: 5 h 5 m 14 servings 240 calories (each, not in 6 to 8 total)

Ingredients:
1 .25 oz. package active dry yeast
½ cup warm water (105 degrees F/41degrees C)
2 ½ tablespoons white sugar (I added more for taste)
½ cup milk
2 tablespoons butter, melted
1 teaspoon vanilla extract
1 large egg
1/8 teaspoon freshly grated nutmeg (I bought already crushed)
1 lb. all-purpose flour
12 teaspoons low moisture butter) I used regular butter) at
   room temperature and divided

Process Part 1: 4 hours

Place yeast into the mixing bowl of a large stand mixer. Whisk in warm water and let stand until a creamy foam forms on top; about 5 minutes. Add salt, sugar, milk, 2 tablespoons melted butter, vanilla extract, egg, and nutmeg. Whisk mixture thoroughly. Pour flour on top of liquid ingredients. Place mixing bowl onto mixer.

1. Attach dough hook to mixer and knead on low speed until dough comes together in a ball and becomes soft and sticky, about 3 minutes. Dough will stick to the hook and pull away from the side of the bowl.
2. Transfer dough to a floured work surface, knead 2 or 3 times, and shape into a ball. Wrap dough in plastic and refrigerate for 20 minutes to let gluten relax.
3. Remove dough from refrigerator, unwrap, and dust lightly with flour. Roll out into a 9x18-inch rectangle about 1/4 inch thick. Evenly spread 6 tablespoons softened unsalted

butter onto the middle third of the dough. Fold one unbuttered third over the buttered third and press lightly; spread remaining 6 tablespoons of unsalted button on top of that third. Fold remaining third over the first (buttered) third. Transfer dough onto a sheet pan, cover lightly with plastic wrap and a kitchen towel, and refrigerate 20 to 30 more minutes for butter to become firm. Sprinkle dough lightly with flour as you work if it becomes sticky.

4. Return dough to floured work surface and pat very gently into an 8x14 rectangle about 1/2-inch thick. Fold outer thirds over center third as before; roll out into an 8x14-inch rectangle again. Keep edges of rectangle as straight as possible. Fold in thirds as before. Cover dough lightly with a kitchen towel, and refrigerate for 2 hours.

5. Roll the dough out to about 3/8 inch thick. Cut dough in half crosswise. Leave half on a lightly floured work surface; refrigerate other half of dough until needed.

6. Use a sharp 3-inch circular cutter to cut 8 circles of dough from piece on the work surface. Use 1-inch size cutter to cut the donut holes out of the dough circles.

7. Line a baking sheet with waxed paper and sprinkle lightly with flour. Arrange cronuts and holes onto prepared baking sheet. Let rise in a draft-free, warm place (such as an unheated oven) until doubled in size, about 1 hour.

Process Part 2: 2 hours thirty minutes
Ingredients:
6 cups oil (or more as needed)
1 cup confectioner's sugar
½ teaspoon milk (or as needed)
½ teaspoon vanilla extract

1. Once dough has been made, cut, and dough has risen (see How to Make Cronuts, Part1) continue on to fry and glaze your homemade cronuts.

2. Heat vegetable oil in a deep fryer or a deep saucepan over medium heat to 350 degrees F (175 degrees C).

3. Carefully lift a cronut and gently drop into oil. Fry 2 at a time until golden brown, 1 1/2 to 2 minutes per side. Cronuts will puff up as they cook. Drain on racks over paper towels; let cool.

4. Whisk confectioners' sugar, milk, and vanilla extract in a shallow bowl until glaze is smooth and slightly runny.

5. Pick up a fried cronut and gently dip the top in glaze; return to rack and let stand until glaze has set, about 15 minutes.

6. Alternate version: For higher-rising cronuts, roll out finished dough (see Part I) into an 8x12 inch rectangle. Fold dough in thirds and roll out into a rectangle about 3/4 inch thick. Cut out 6 cronuts and holes, using a 3-inch round cutter and a 1-inch small hole cutter.

7. Line baking sheet with waxed paper and dust paper lightly with flour. Place cronuts and holes onto prepared baking sheet and let rise in a draft-free place until doubled, about 1 hour.

8. Carefully pick up and gently drop cronuts, 2 at a time, into the preheated oil. Fry 1 1/2 to 2 minutes per side. The extra fold and making the dough thicker will result in taller cronuts than before. Let fried cronuts drain on racks.

9. Dip tops of cronuts in glaze as described above, and let cool on racks to let glaze set up.

Expanding to Embrace the Hispanic Culture – Chilies Rellenos upon Request

Nellie Galaviz was one of the full-time employees responsible for checking residents in and out Residence Inn. I believe she was the youngest employees and had responsibility for providing general services at check-in. Shortly after she started working there, she wanted to know, "When are you going to make us some Hispanic dishes"? I had little experience in that genre and had purposefully avoided creating any of them in the past because I felt they were meals the locals ate all the time, so why would I try to match their expertise? I asked Nellie why she suggested I create menus from her culture and she replied, "We want to see if you can really cook, after all we don't know what the food from your culture should taste like." This young woman had spunk. OK, it made sense to me, so I asked what they would like me to prepare. I assumed it would be something fairly simple like tacos or fajitas. I had seen them cooked in restaurants several times and they didn't look difficult to prepare as long as I followed a recipe.

It was suggested that I demonstrate my true ability as a chef and prepare Chilies Rellenos. I had no idea what she was talking about, and rather than admit my ignorance, I said, "Sure, that should be easy." Little did I know that I was in for the most difficult challenge I had faced to date. Preparing this meal required I learned new techniques of controlling the temperature of hot oil in a frying pan. I began my research and discovered that Chilies Rellenos is a Mexican dish consisting of stuffed peppers dipped in a light egg batter and delicately fried to perfection. It originated in the city of Puebla, Mexico and it is not an easy dish to prepare properly. What a challenge I had found myself into that day. I am not a delicate person. I knew that I was going to have to choose an authentic chilies rellenos recipe and nothing less would be unacceptable. This was not enough time to attempt an experiment, so by the books was the plan.

With printed recipe from Allrecipies.com in hand, I went to the Ralph's ® to purchase the ingredients that until that day some of which were unknown to me: Anaheim Chili peppers, baking powder, Queso Fresco cheese, eggs and flour. I had the oil for my fried chicken dinners. I was surprised there were such few ingredients and figured it was going to be easier than I thought. That is, until I read the process steps that made the preparation and construction of the dish difficult.

Simply speaking (trust me it was far from easy) these are the steps in making authentic Chilies Rellenos:

1. Blister and peel Anaheim peppers (first two attempts I burned the peppers)
2. Slit cooled and skinned peppers and remove seeds
3. Dry peppers and stuff with strips of Queso Fresco cheese
4. Separate egg yolk from egg whites and beat both separate
5. Fold gently beaten egg whites into whipped egg yolks
6. Roll stuffed peppers in flour and dip in egg mixture
7. Fry peppers in one cup of oil on medium heat until lightly golden brown for about 5 minutes per side to ensure cheese has melted (watch carefully to avoid burning)
8. Add additional egg mixture to cover peppers in pan before flipping to second side
9. Line fried chilies in a pan or casserole dish and cover with a chunky crushed tomato-based sauce that has been cooked down with crushed garlic and ground dried oregano.
10. Top peppers with mixed Mexican cheese and put in a 350-degree oven for twenty minutes or until cheese is melted.

My first attempt at Chilies Rellenos
Not bad for a rookie

After burning one set of peppers beyond recognition while setting off the fire alarm in my room, then overcooking two stuffed peppers (scorched) in the oil, I managed to reach an acceptable level of cooking temperature. The resultant success was 8 fried peppers that appeared to be within a reasonably acceptable standard. I rushed downstairs with the Chilies Relleno and watched as the staff savored, smiled and applauded my efforts. They declared me to be a true chef and never asked again to see my credentials. Although, on every other occasion that I prepared food for the staff it did not seem to matter; whatever I prepared they devoured and asked for more.

When I selected my first Chilies Rellenos recipe I chose to use Ancho/Pasilla peppers. Since that day, I learned that locally and across the Southwest, people also use Hatch Green Chilies, Anaheim pepper and Poblano peppers. I tried all of these varieties and prefer the Poblano because of the extra heat they provide. When inviting guests, I inquire of their tolerance to 'heat' levels before selecting my chilies to become Rellenos.

Process Improvement – Chilies Rellenos Casserole – there had to be an easier way

I had discovered that time and energy are two important elements to conserve. Therefore, I decided that though I loved the results and delicious taste that traditional Chilies Rellenos it was a difficult dish for me to prepare. The process of cooking the stuffed peppers on a bed of frothy egg whites that required a precisely controlled temperature of the oil, and having time for the cooking period, and then to have to flip the stuffed peppers over in the oil and cooking without being able to check doneness of the interior of the peppers provided me many opportunities for monumental failure. I enjoyed creating dishes that are repeatable and can be prepared without disastrous results. I discovered that casseroles, stews and slow cooked meats are easier for the average cook to recreate, prepare successfully the first time, and avoid spending the entire day in the kitchen.

Though I was somewhat successful in my first attempt at Chilies Rellenos and I continued to make them on occasion, I determined that there I must seek an alternative solution to such a delicate process. A few months after my first attempt I proceeded to experiment with variations of Chilies Rellenos that incorporated my new-found understanding of the savory elements of the dish and turned to my Italian heritage for a viable solution.

After several unsatisfying attempts, my final thoughts were to take the theme and taste of Chilies Relleno and expand from there to create a new combination of the same ingredients into Eric's Chilies Rellenos Casserole. I prepared the dish, ate a large portion myself, declared it a personal success that was ready to be introduced to the world of culinary expert judges. On to the expert tasting with my friends, the hotel staff. I made sure it was an evening that Nellie was working the front desk since this part of my journey began with her request. The early reviews came back with high marks for creativity, taste and originality.

Everyone questioned how I had come up with the idea of creating a Chilies Rellenos Casserole that looked suspiciously like a tomato-based lasagna.

I discovered that the Chilies Rellenos Casserole I created required far more preparation time in the kitchen that the traditional Chilies Rellenos cooked in a frying pan. However, the repeatability of process and confidence in my skills made the creation far more plausible and became incorporated into my repertoire of dishes.

Chilies Rellenos Casserole

Food Channel Revisited – To Quote Jim Valvano, "Don't ever give up …"

I felt growing confidence in my culinary skills after creating the Chilies Rellenos Casserole and decided to share it with the world. The Food Chanel had a series of contests sponsored by Sargento where each quarter home chefs would create their favorite main dish using specific ingredients and incorporate Sargento cheese. The contest required that the chef described their dish, provided the recipe and pictures of the finished product. The first in the series of quarterly contests was to create a Mexican/Hispanic dish.

I had convinced myself that my new creation, Chilies Rellenos Casserole would absolutely be the winner and enthusiastically submitted my unique application; pictures and all. The prized was to be that the winner would be selected to appear on the Chopped series and participate as a competitor. Alas, my creation was bested by other mouth-watering entries. Therefore, I was "Chopped" again, even before I started.

From the Food Channel competition experience for the following Quarterly submission, I chose and adaptation intended to create a Low-Carb recipe using cauliflower. This is what I created and submitted as my entry:

Chili Relleno Casserole (low carb recipe)
by Eric Pearson 2/21/2016

Ingredients:

½ head shredded cauliflower	2 cups shredded Sargento® sharp cheddar cheese
3 stalk leeks	8 ounces cremini mushrooms (thinly sliced)
9 large Anaheim peppers	6 eggs – separated

½ cup sesame oil or virgin olive oil	2 cloves fresh garlic, minced
1 tablespoon ground cumin	2 teaspoon paprika
2 tablespoon course sea salt	1tablespoon pepper
1/3 cup all-purpose flour	1 cup 2% milk

Directions:

Prep

1. Grill /fire Anaheim peppers to scorch skin, place in plastic bag and sweat skins, remove skins, cut stem end and toss, split pepper / remove seeds and two strings. Open flat and cut into four equal sections

2. Cut fresh cauliflower head in half, remove core and stems. Shred florets (or chop finely) lightly salt and pepper, add paprika. Cook cauliflower in 2 teaspoons of medium hot oil, folding carefully to heat and lightly brown cauliflower. Proper cooking results in rice consistency pieces. Set aside. Serves as low carb substitute for rice

3. Slice thinly 8 ounces of Cremini mushrooms; lightly oil, add crushed/minced garlic and ground cumin. Cook in 2 teaspoons oil until mushrooms are warm and limp. Drain water and set aside

4. Clean and cut three stalks of leeks. Remove dark green leaves and cut roots off stem. Slice stalks and soak 10 minutes in lightly salt water. Steam leeks in ½ cup water for 8 minutes separate. Set aside

5. Separate 6 eggs into two bowls; whites and yolks. Set aside

6. Softly mix egg yolks with salt & pepper to taste then mix with 1 cup milk and 1/3 cup flower. Set aside

7. Whip egg whites to fluffy and beginning of peaks. Set aside

8. Lightly oil 2- or 3-quart glass baking dish and preheat oven to 350 degrees

Assembly

1. Place one layer of Anaheim peppers on bottom of baking dish, alternately reversing wide end to balance peppers
2. Add 1/2 of Cremini mushrooms on top of pepper
3. Add one ½ of cauliflower on top of mushrooms
4. Add ½ of shredded Sargento® sharp cheese on top of cauliflower
5. Pour 1/ of mixed egg yolks on layer and allow to soak in
6. Repeat previous 5 steps creating 2nd layer
7. Add whipped egg whites to top of casserole and carefully fold into top layer.

Baking

1. Place casserole on baking sheet and place on center rack in preheated 350 degree oven for 1 hour and 15 minutes until top is crusty and center in moist but dry when checked with knife or wooden toothpick
2. Remove from oven and let stand 10 minutes.

Serving

To serve use a flat bladed spatula, first separate casserole from sides of glass baking dish and then carefully cut into squares or rectangles. Remove sections one at a time, plate and serve hot.

You can create a two-layer casserole consisting of the following sub-layers: grilled Anaheim peppers, grilled shredded cauliflower, sauté Cremini mushrooms in paprika, hot mustard and crushed garlic, sliced & steamed leeks lightly salted, shredded Sargento sharp cheddar cheese, add in 6 mixed egg yolks with 1 cup milk and 1/3 cup flour.

Last step, pour and fold in 6 whipped egg whites into top layer. Casserole is of a soufflé consistency. Prep each item set aside and then assemble two layers in greased glass baking dish and put in 350-degree oven. Bake for one hour and fifteen minutes. Let stand five to ten minutes, and remember to separate casserole from sides of dish, cut in sections and serve like lasagna with a light side salad and a glass of red wine.

My Chills Relleno Casserole Bake
Food Chanel Submittal

Tacos, Taquitos & Enchiladas –
Food Truck Specials

Once I had accepted and semi-mastered the challenge of Chilies Rellenos in addition to having created the Chilies Rellenos Casserole that everyone raved about, I decided it was time to completely immerse myself into the local Mexican/Hispanic culture and build my repertoire and learn to cook as many different ethnic dishes possible. My expansion into the local Southern California experience led me to developing my own recipes for the following:

1. Tacos
2. Taquitos
3. Enchiladas
4. Ceviche
5. El Pollo Loco
6. Fajitas
7. Empanadas
8. Quesadillas
9. Chile con Queso
10. Chicken Tortilla Soup
11. Guacamole
12. Huevos Rancheros
13. Nachos
14. Tamales
15. Empanadas

Deep Fried Mini-Burrito

I had begun with virtually no knowledge of Hispanic foods and quickly increased my ethnic culinary skills, one dish at a time. I concentrated on "South of the Boarder" selections. Previously my skills in this genre only offered me the ability to order dinner at Qdoba and El Polo Loco chicken or from street taco vendors by pointing at the pictures because the menus were all written in Spanish.

Breakfast Pork with an International Flavor

Having always been confident when cooking large portions of meat, I intended to have leftovers for quick dishes during the work-week. My leftovers most often became repurposed rather than just warming a plate in the microwave of the same entree from the previous night. Here I share two of my breakfast creations using "the other white meat," pork. Leftovers, never again shall we use that word. I guess this makes me environmentally conscious.

Scrambled eggs, fried pork cutlets and polenta was created to make use of leftover center cut, boneless pork roast, dry rubbed with a personal mixture, cooked at 375 degrees for two hours and sliced thin like bacon. It was then pan fried at medium heat with minimal oil until warm throughout. Another addition to the meal was French bread toast with butter and homemade strawberry jam.

Pulled pork Boston butt with chopped onions and pork stock
4 scrambled eggs
Queso dip for on top
Sliced Jalapenos as a garnish (and heat in every bite)
Bread and butter to soak up the juices and to balance the heat

Scrambled Eggs, fried pork cutlets, polenta

Pulled pork, scrambled eggs, Queso dip

Feed One or Feed Fifty – It's all the same to me, I never sacrifice quality for quantity

I had developed my skills at creating Hispanic dishes. I was (always have been) an outspoken person who spoke to everyone and was able to get to know the entire hotel staff, not just the management and desk services people. I started by feeding the employees a bit at a time. When I created a new tasty tidbit, I quickly wandered around the hotel property and offered warm bites to the staff as they made their way through their daily duties. The French call them hors d'oeuvres, fancy for appetizers. Since I requested that my room be serviced only once a week instead of daily, I would often stop the cleaning staff and trade towels and linins once or twice a week and occasionally pick up extra paper towels and shampoo at the same time. I used those opportunities and offered them something to eat in exchange. Anytime I needed something, there was always someone willing to stop what they were doing and respond favorably. In life we all too often live in our own private world and fail to reach out to others who look, and act different.

After being at the Residence Inn for six months, I felt fully integrated in my cooking skills, plus having also procured most of my kitchen tools as well as having learned to prepare Hispanic fare, it was time for real action. I took a deep breath and offered to prepare a luncheon for the entire hotel staff, including the forty-five women and men who cleaned the rooms and maintained the facilities. Of the staff, only four men worked at the hotel. I was surrounded by a facility full of hard-working women.

The luncheon was planned for a Friday from 11:30 A.M. – 1:00 P.M. That allowed me the previous weekend to plan the meal, purchase the food and begin the prep well ahead of time. I did most of the cooking in the evenings. I spent the rest of the week preparing the selections, marinating and precooking some of the entrees and finally completing the preparations. Beginning at 5:00 A.M. on Friday morning I pulled the entire luncheon together. After the morning breakfast service, I was allowed to use the hotel kitchen for the final prep and setup. Then I served the luncheon in the dining arear reserved for the resident breakfast and dinner buffet. I lined the counter with pots and pans of food, crock pots and steamers of rice and meats, and set up a buffet that had taken me more than fifty hours to prepare and serve.

I lined the buffet bar with the numerous entrees, salads and appetizers and waited for my fifty +/- guests to arrive. We enjoyed a great lunch, there was lots of chatter in Spanish of which I understood little to none, but it was accompanied with many smiles, hugs and thank you(s). The luncheon was a success and it became an event I looked forward to providing three times a year until I retired. I asked for no special favors from the hotel staff during my stay. However, I did have the run of the facilities and on cleaning day, my room was well appointed and spotlessly clean upon my arrival after a day at work.

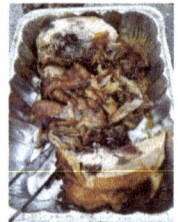

Chef Eric offering Jerk Chicken and Carolina Pulled Pork

Celebrating a holiday meal with the Residence Inn cleaning staff

When East Meets South – Combining Culinary Delights

As I began to meet more people from different cultures, I enhanced my journey developing alternate ethnic dishes that I had never embraced in my early years as a novice cook. I realized that the best way to introduce one culture to another was to offer a blend of favorites by combining rather than shoving a completely different meal on someone, and have their first impression be a visual of something they might not be willing to try. I had never appreciated the appearance of slimy okra (a staple in the Southern United States) or the taste of Brussel sprouts (look like tiny cabbages and often boiled to death).

Since I was a resident of EL Segundo, California and the local fare included a large variety of Hispanic dishes, I decided my first endeavor of an Ethnic Combo Meal would be to create a Carolina Pork BBQ taco. My initial attempt was such a success that I never varied from the recipe after the first meal with Carolina pork as the featured ingredient. These can be just as easily prepared as soft or hard tacos, thought this picture shows the soft tortilla shell and the basket of flavors delivered.

Having provided the Carolina Pork BBQ recipe and obligatory pictures elsewhere in addition to the fact that everyone can make a taco, I am only including the ingredients and a picture for your drooling pleasure. Besides, the best part of making tacos is to include your own favorite ingredients once you select your meat or vegetarian based desire.

Carolina Pork Tacos Recipe ingredients:
Well-seasoned and slow cooked Carolina pork
Soft/hard taco shells, tortillas or even blended in an enchilada style blanket pf spices and cheeses
Kentucky Fried Chicken coleslaw (no lettuce required)
Sliced/chopped Roma or tomatillo tomatoes (how authentic do you desire to be)

Shredded five variety of cheeses
Chopped onions
Cilantro
Dash of salt and pepper
Picante sauce
Sliced/chopped Jalapeño peppers
Your favorite hot sauce
Go heavy on the pork and add the hot sauce in moderation

Carolina Port BBQ Soft Tacos
Twice cooked and pan roasted

"Meals on Demand" became commonplace for the Residence Inn Staff

As mentioned, previous, I spent my weekends buying ingredients and doing my sous chef preparations; slicing and dicing and stocking the fridge for the week ahead. The hotel staff had quickly become knowledgeable of my schedule and abilities and increased the frequency of their 4:00 p.m. question when I arrived home after working since 6:00 a.m. "What do you have for dinner"? Off I would go to my room and re-appear thirty to forty-five minutes later with the special of the day.

One such easy to prepare meal and relatively close to traditional Hispanic fare was my deep-fried pork taquitos that looked more like egg rolls because I wrapped the ends to keep the ingredients from falling out during the cooking process. Traditional taquitos are thin only filled with meat and/or cheese and rolled, not wrapped in a corn tortilla and most often baked.

Corn tortilla shell, shredded pork BBQ, shredded cheese, chopped spring onions, cottage cheese, pimentos, chopped celery, sliced tomatoes on the side

Another last-minute preparation the Residence Inn Staff enjoyed was my ground beef soft taco on a grilled flour tortilla shell. These delights consisted of: fresh ground beef cooked with selected spices, chopped Poblano and/or Anaheim peppers, marinated and sautéed mushrooms, diced lettuce, chopped tomatoes and shredded Mexican cheese. I often added additional chilies and hot spices to the ones I prepared for myself.

Ground beef soft tacos, a Wednesday night delight

A little Spring year-round – Vietnamese Spring Rolls

In the effort to learn more styles, regional favorites and investigate ways to use leftovers by repurposing, I continued to investigate different cultures. I discovered moist rice papers in the Ralph's grocery store one day. I bought a package and headed back to the hotel to do some research and experimentation. I discovered that there are two standard ways to make Vietnamese spring rolls. Traditionally they are fresh and not cooked and more often than not use fresh vegetables, but also meat on occasion. I tried both; cooked and uncooked as well as with and without meat. I was hungry during the experimental session and ended up eating all of the uncooked ones while preparing the deep-fried version. I found that spring rolls worked well for a light snack, Fairley easy to prepare and an excellent way to repurpose my chopped and diced vegetables. The addition to vegetables only, was accomplished by adding the leftover pulled pork or jerk chicken.

For me, the most important part of the process when frying the spring rolls was to make sure the oil in my cooking vessel was at the correct temperature. I avoided putting too many rolls in at the same time. Just like fried chicken, donuts, or French fries the temperature will drop significantly and the rice paper will absorb the oil and detract from the crisp bite experience and the low-calorie results intended. After each pan was browned, I allowed the oil to return to the optimal temperature before adding the next batch of spring rolls. I desired a consistent and medium heat, then gently flipped the rolls to ensure both sides turned a golden brown; approximately 5 minutes total. Cooking on high as most people do with their fried chicken will quickly burn the rice paper and the filling will remain cool or barley warm.

Fresh Vegetable & Shrimp Spring Rolls

Not everything is filled with meat: Vegetable Spring Roll Appetizer
Both cooked and uncooked provided pleasure to the palate

The metamorphosis of leftovers to become tasty deep fried spring rolls. Instead of describing the process I'll demonstrate through pictures. Note, I used a shallow frying pan rather than heat up my deep fryer.

Serve with your favorite sauces, light, thick, mid or spicy
I prefer to offer five different sauces

Baked chicken with muffin bread stuffing – A Sunday Favorite

We forget that we have muffin/cupcake pans in our cupboard and they see seldom use. I hope this recipe inspires others to venture outside of the pastry side of muffin tins.

A meal that I always found easy to prepare was baked chicken stuffed with apples, celery and onions. I added a side of bread or cornbread-based stuffing cooked in muffin pans with lots of butter. These were easy to store (they can be frozen for three months) and reheated; one or two at a time. In addition, the necessary accoutrement to finish of a well-balanced meal was home-made chicken gravy. Add your choice of an in-season green vegetable, summer squash or mashed potatoes.

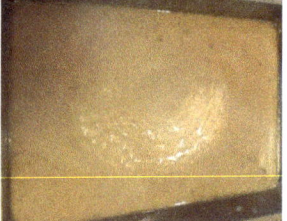

Baked, apple and celery stuffed chicken with muffin bread stuffing
Chicken Gravy goes with everything and tastes like chicken

I prepared and laid out the planning for the entire week's meals on Saturday or Sunday. After everything was complete and set out on the counter, I would then plate individual servings for the staff. When they requested a bite to eat during the evening shift, I would pull everything out of the refrigerator, prepare or reheat individual dishes to ensure proper temperature and then load the individual plates for the staff.

I learned my plating techniques from The Food Channel – clean and neat

Beef chuck roast mashed potatoes & gravy
with a side of avocado

Sliced Tri-tip and roasted chicken
on soft taco shells with avocado

Baked chicken pieces smothered in gravy
With a side of mashed potatoes and gravy

*New York Ribeye, steamed spinach,
sautéed mushrooms & twice baked potato*

Crock pot lasagna and a side of toasted garlic bread

*Cornish hens, fresh bacon topped garden salad
and steamed green beans*

During one weekend I decided to test out a new crockpot recipe on myself, and of course the evening staff on duty. They were my captured audience and seldom turned down a free meal. Slow cooking options offered me far more capabilities to prepare a dinner entrée while working a long shift every day. I prepared the ingredients ahead of time, marinated the meat for two to three days, assembles the meal and put the crockpot on low power. One can also prepare many of these types of meals by cooking in the oven at 180 to 200 degrees. This recipe was one of many I had pulled off the internet and adapted to my style of cooking using available ingredients. My next endeavor was to try my hand at crockpot spinach lasagna.

I prepared it just like any other lasagna dish with the noodles sauce, spinach, ricotta cheese (one can substitute large curd cottage cheese) and spices. I layered it the same way I had typically created lasagna and put it on low for the long soak cooking process. I let it cool slightly, topped with freshly shredded Romano or Parmesan cheese, scooped and served.

Crockpot Spinach Lasagna and garlic bread

Mama Mia – Five (5) Kinds of Lasagna

As we investigate and experience the people and the foods of different cultures and sub-cultures, we find that there are many ways to build a better meal through experimentation and experience. In addition, the rage to replace meat products with vegetables, rice with grilled cauliflower and gluten free products for wheat and pastas, has created an explosion in the transformation of your grandmother's lasagna as well as many other family favorites.

In my travels and love for experimentation I have tried several options for lasagna including meatless as well as using different cooking vessels. I found a recipe for crock-pot lasagna and had to try to recreate it. The most exciting element was that once I filled the crock-pot with the ingredients, I was able to walk away and come back hours later to a delicious pot full of an Italian favorite that had slowly cooked all day in my absence.

As the pictures below demonstrate, I have made at least five different variations of this family favorite:

1. Traditional with lasagna noodles, marinara sauce, ground beef, fresh tomatoes, five different cheeses and a baked crust, to die for (or is it, for which to die).
2. Spinach lasagna with the normal ingredients of noodles and meatless marinara sauce; spinach replaced the meat.
3. Crock-pot lasagna (noted above)
4. Zucchini lasagna where the pasta noodles are replaced by thin-sliced zucchini (I forgot to take a picture, but the completed dish looks like all the others until you cut it into squares and serve.
5. Chilies Relleno Casserole. This was not intended to be a variety of lasagna, however when I created the casserole in lieu of the traditional fried Chilies Rellenos, I constructed it and baked it the same as I had all of my lasagna dishes.

Traditional Lasagna   *Spinach Lasagna*

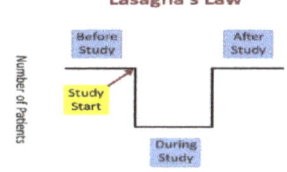

Lasagna's Law

Number of Patients

Before Study

After Study

Study Start

During Study

"The number of patients available to join a trial drops by 90% the day a trial begins.
They re-appear as soon as the study is over."

Crock-pot Lasagna   *Zucchini Lasagna*
                                       (forgot the pictures)

Chilies Relleno - Lasagna style

Corned Beef – Crockpot style

Another favorite easy to prepare, one pot meal is corned beef, potatoes and carrots. I must admit that I should have selected a smaller portion of corned beef. In this effort, my cup runneth over. And yes, for the highly observant, the recipe required ½ a can of beer and trust me the other half was not wasted. I used red potatoes because they hold up better than Idaho or Russet potatoes in a slow-cook recipe.

Corned Beef slow cooked in the crock pot *Beef stock, onions, red potatoes, carrots, ½ can beer (yes, I grew up on Miller High Life)*

The Food Channel – My On-Air Training Classes

Once I had settled in my studio (a.k.a, 424 sq. ft. hotel room), I began to watch many hours each night of The Food Channel® and became hooked on the Chopped Series. The nightly ritual kept me off the streets at night and enhanced my cooking skills with each episode I devoured. I inhaled delicate and exotic terms for simple operations in the kitchen like 'roux' instead of 'gravy'. My grandmother, Lillian Pearson from Wilson, North Carolina prepared many a meal for the Pearson Clan several times a year. I can't remember her ever calling it anything other than gravy: gravy boat, sausage and gravy, mashed potatoes and gravy, biscuits and gravy. Sometimes we substituted molasses and clear country ham gravy for the standard white gravy. No matter, it was always called gravy in her house. As they say, "It's all gravy to me."

The Chopped Series is a scripted program where four budding or accomplished chefs participate in a three round, loser out competition to make: 1) An appetizer, 2) a main meal and 3) a dessert. At the conclusion of each of the three rounds one of the chef contestants is eliminated until there is 'one chef standing'.

The time allowed for each round is always limited to twenty or thirty minutes and participants are required to incorporate four seldom complementary secret ingredients from within a basket situated on the cooking station. The chefs must incorporate all of the mystery ingredients in the dish (generally four) as well as highlight them in a significant way. Can't see it, can't taste it, you lose big time.

I learned by observing that survival on the Chopped series and especially Cutthroat Kitchen was more about avoiding mistakes and meeting short time deadlines than actual preparation of amazing meals that normally took hours to prepare. Presentation and incorporation of the four main ingredients is the key to success on this show. If you have little time to cook dinner, then I suggest you study Chopped on the Food Channel, like I did for three years and begin experimenting on your own. I guarantee your results will suffer the first several times you attempt what you see on the television however, success will prevail.

One must also have great 'knife skills' and maintain a safe and clean kitchen. I have seen more quality chefs get chopped because they cut a finger during the rush to complete, causing their great creations to be inedible and therefore disqualified from competition. Practice, practice and more practice and you will have developed a repertoire of quick meals with tasty choices in you inventory of: appetizers, main courses and desserts.

Because there was an addictive nature to the show, and my desire to be ready for my dream of the call to appear as a competitor, I had purchased in addition to the basics in all kitchens, the following spices that so far, I have been unable to create the appropriate dish that would have forced me to crack their seal.

Unused Spices in my inventory:

1. Chinese Five Spice
2. Cardamom
3. Citrus Chili & Garlic with CHIA
4. Dill Weed
5. Cinnamon Sticks
6. Fennell Seeds
7. Caraway Seeds
8. Arrowroot
9. Mediterranean Spice Blend
10. Pumpkin Pie Spice
11. ANCHO Chili Pepper
12. Black Garlic Powder
13. Tarragon Leaves
14. Saffron
15. Ginger (cracked)
16. Hibiscus Flowers
17. Start Anise
18. Juniper Berries (ground)

The Food Channel Revisited – I'll never give up

I discovered that "Third time's the charm" didn't work for me. In completing my research for this book, I found it necessary to review the application process and requirements for consideration to become a contestant. Upon arriving at the site, I was immediately drawn to the current 'call for chefs'; professional and non-professionals, moms and dads, teenagers and kids. Strictly for the purpose of research I reviewed the application for non-professionals and decided it was time to give the Food Channel a fourth opportunity to review my updated application therefore, I subsequently applied one more time for consideration.

Stay tuned, perhaps before I have completed the book, I'll be able to share my experience on Chopped for Dads, Backyard Grillers, possibly new category Hotel Residents, or perhaps real old people who can't remember the proper measures for any dessert recipe.

Pass the Salt and Pepper Please

For those who believe that cooking is a "Sunday Walk in the Park" for example there are twelve different types of salt for cooking and each has a different purpose:

1. Table Salt
2. Kosher Salt
3. Sea Salt
4. Himalayan Pink Salt
5. Fleur de Sel ($16/lb.)
6. Kala Namak
7. Flake Salt
8. Black Hawaiian Salt
9. Red Hawaiian Salt
10. Smoked Salt
11. Pickling Salt

I must share one recommendation passed to me by a wise chef who had shared his wisdom with me several times. "If you are eating a meal, please taste the food before dousing it with salt, pepper, hot sauce, ketchup … It just might have been prepared to match the most discerning palate and shows disrespect to your host to load it down with condiments." Yes, I know what you are thinking, and I too often receive the generic comment, "But, I always add salt and pepper to my food." Just don't do it before tasting the dish.

Cooking Trivia Questions

What are the seven most expensive spices by weight?

1. Saffron (stigma of the Crocus Sativus flower) $5,000/lb.
2. Vanilla Bean $200/lb.
3. Cardamom $30/lb.
4. Clove $10/lb.
5. Cinnamon $6/lb.
6. Pepper $3/lb.
7. Turmeric $3/lb.

Bonus Question: Is salt the cheapest spice?
Bonus Question Answer:

Salt, although readily available and extremely inexpensive is a mineral, not a spice, therefore the correct answer is No, but not because of its cost or availability in the marketplace. That leaves pepper as the cheapest and most frequently used spice by weight and price. However, don't expect to get exotic peppercorn cheap or the fancy bottled 2 oz. size in your favorite store for less than fifty cents. Buy in small quantities unless you are on your way to becoming a professional chef.

Pepper is called 'the king of spice' with a long history of being used as a seasoning, a preservative and in some cultures as currency to trade for other goods and services. It comes in three colors; black, white and green and is best used when freshly ground; so, make sure you own a good peppermill.

From Cricket to American Football – Closing the Divide as East Meets West

One of my early introductions to four young gentlemen from India became a lesson for all of us, one I enjoy sharing whenever I can. I met these young men when I stopped in the dining area of the Residence Inn one evening during dinner. They were sitting by themselves and speaking Hindi while they ate fresh fruit, bread, rice and beans. For breakfast I had noticed they generally ate fruit, dry toast and oatmeal. It appeared that all of them were Vegetarians.

I only learned that they were speaking Hindi after I introduced myself and asked about this language I did not understand. I quickly discovered that the #1 foreign language spoken by Indian people is English followed by French. My two years of French studies in high school some fifty years previous had left me useless in that area of conversation. I also learned from our many discussions, there are hundreds of languages commonly spoken in India where approximately 41% of the people speak Hindi as their first language.

After introductions and two evening of dinner conversations I learned that all four of these young men were from Central India, had completed an undergraduate degree in Chemistry in India and came to The United States to complete a Masters' degree in Quality Assurance at New Jersey Institute of Technology in Newark, New Jersey. They had graduated and were working as Quality Assurance professionals for one of the soap manufacturers in Los Angeles, California on work visas. If you are old enough you might recognize the company the television commercial with Madge the manicurist from 1967, "You're Soaking in It". She represented Palmolive dish detergent.

The guys asked me if I ate Indian food and upon responding with a resounding yes, they invited me to join them at a local Indian Buffet the following Sunday. The most obvious and striking observation I noticed upon entering the restaurant was that other than the waiters and chefs, my hosts for lunch were the only people of Indian descent in the restaurant. Noticing the look on my face, they reassured me that this restaurant was the most authentic Indian food in the area and I would not leave disappointed. I ate some of everything while they only ate dishes without meat.

When the check came, I grabbed for it as I all along had planned to pay for all of us. Sai pulled the bill out of my hand and explained that when you were an invited guest in India, you paid for nothing as it was an honor to share all they have with others. That was a great lesson I learned about their culture from this simple experience. I immediately invited them to come for lunch the following Sunday in my make-shift kitchen/living room/bedroom and offered to explain to them the game of American Football as we watched a National Football League (NFL) Sunday game. They had never watched NFL football so this was going to be a new experience for all of us.

Having never cooked traditional Indian food and completely missing saffron and curry in my spice inventory I had to spend three evenings researching foods and one evening shopping for the appropriate ingredients that were missing from my cupboard. To complicate my efforts, all four gentlemen were practicing vegetarians. Three of them were as you might say 'rail thin' and the other one kind of heavy. I had to wonder, but never asked, "What was the one eating the other three weren't"?

By the next Sunday and after three days of preparation, I provided a balanced meal and covered the entire range of flavors from mild to hot and from sweet to sour. My research had indicated I was obligated to provide different textures: crunchy, soft, dry, moist, rough and smooth. Lest I forget to offer some dishes hot while others chilled. And remember, no meat.

I served the following meal at 1:00 P.M. as we watched their first National Football League game:

1. Cauliflower and potato curry
2. White rice

3. Jalapeno Saffron rice
4. Coconut rice
5. Chana dal
6. Papaya
7. Gobi Aloo
8. Curry potatoes with chilies and peas
9. Coriander and tamarind chutney
10. Challah bread, Naan bread
11. Coconut rice pudding

We spread the consumption of the meal out to cover pre-game, halftime, fourth quarter and after game dessert. Upon completion of the meal and their first NFL football game they asked two questions:

Q. How did you learn to cook traditional Indian dishes so well?
A. I am developing my skills as a Chef and spent a week practicing.

Q. Why is the one guy on the field always putting his hand under the other players butt?
A. The quarterback reaches between the legs of the center to receive the ball; called the hike which begins each play from the line of scrimmage.

We became good friends that day and by the end of the season they had taken a hiatus from Cricket as we celebrated the NFL Super Bowl together; where I served a fully vegetarian American fare to their delight.

Would You Like a Cup of Tea?

I met Pari (meaning angel, fairy or princess) when she joined my new friends from India. She had recently arrived from New Jersey Tech to work with them. She was quiet, always spoke with a soft voice and mostly kept to herself. She never watched an NFL football game with us on Sunday, Sunday night, Thursday night or Monday Night Football. I guess she was committed to the game of cricket, though they said she read a lot of books and wasn't very social.

My daughter Erika came to California for a week to visit and experience some of the Los Angeles sights. We decided to take a tour of the beautiful and historic Getty Villa at 17985 Pacific Coast Highway in Pacific Palisades, California, just about a half-hour drive up the coast from my long-term home at the Residence Inn. We invited Pari to join us and explained the history and significance of the museum.

I reminded Pari that we had an appointment time issued by the museum that they used to control the number of people in the facilities at one time and we needed to leave no later than 10:00 A.M. Because no one could ever predict the Los Angeles traffic on the 404 and we did not want to arrive late and lose our spot, the departure time was firm. We were required to arrive within fifteen minutes of our appointment time or we could be denied entry. Once on site, you could stay as long as you like.

On the day of the event, I had trouble contacting Pari in her hotel room to remind her of our departure time. She finally answered her phone at 9:45 am and agreed we needed to be on time and asked if we would like a cup of tea before we left. Being polite I said yes and waited for her return call. At 10:30 A.M. she had not called back so I called her and she said she had just finished her shower, needed to get dressed and then tea would be ready.

Again, I reminded her we needed to leave no later than 10:30 am for the Villa and we were already late. I had to explain that we did not have time for tea and asked if she was ready to go and said we would meet her in the hotel lobby at 10:45 am. She finally showed up at 11:00 a.m. and after quick introductions we rushed off to the Getty Villa.

Once we arrived at the Getty, parked the car and walked up the many stairs to the Villa on top of the hill, Pari decided to tour by herself and agreed to meet us in two hours for lunch. The Villa property isn't that expansive, it's only sixty-four acres and most of the property is unavailable for touring, so I figured we were safe with her venturing off on her own. Lunchtime came and went, Pari never showed up so Erika and I had lunch by ourselves. It was my third visit to the Villa and by that time Erika and I had seen everything in the facilities. We were ready to go back to the hotel and began our search for Pari. It was two hours later before she showed up and ready to leave. She said she had decided to skip lunch and ate some apples and nuts she had brought in her purse.

Thinking I had miscommunicated, upon returning to the hotel, I asked the guys if I had misinterpreted some cultural norms and how I could have handled the situation better. They laughed and explained that she was just lazy, slow to do anything, liked to stay by herself and was always late to work. Two weeks later I stopped seeing her around the hotel and they guys explained that she had been fired for poor work attendance and performance and had been shipped back to New Jersey for reassignment.

Camping on the Channel Islands – An extended cooking challenge

Santa Cruz Island is the largest of the Channel Islands off the coast of Southern California. It has many sea caves including the vast Painted Cave, on the northwestern side. The island has many trails, including ones around Scorpion Canyon, with several opportunities to see the island scrub jays. Scorpion Beach features kelp forests. Smugglers Cove and has tide pools. Cavern Point offers Pacific Ocean views and seasonal whale sightings.

Several members of The Bottom Three (B3) Experiential Leadership Group from Northrop Grumman that I had created in 2002 decided we should organize an experiential four-day, three-night camping trip to the Channel Islands off Ventura, California; due West of Los Angeles. The trip required a ferry ride to Santa Cruz Island followed by a half-mile inland trek lugging all of our gear, food and supplies for four days, to the barren camping sites at Scorpion Ranch. We were fortunate that our campsite had several trees in close proximity to each other that provide shade, and opportunity for those of us who wished to sleep in hammocks rather than in tents on the hard ground. Our goal was to camp three nights, hike ten to twenty miles each day, hang-out with good friends, propose solutions to the world's problems, and eat from a well-designed and pre-prepared menu consisting of energy filled calories.

On the way out to the island we were accompanied by several dolphins and a most interesting Sun Fish that must have weighed four-hundred pounds. It appeared to enjoy swimming on its side close to the surface. It was a sight to see and a first for me. The seas were choppy and a drizzle was in the air. Everyone was glad to reach Santa Cruz Island at conclusion of the hour-and-a-half ride.

The campsite that Tim Boyd had reserved included two picnic tables, two bear boxes for storage and several trees growing close together that enabled us to hang five hammocks at varying levels between the trees. We also pitched four tents on the sun-baked ground for those who chose not to sleep elevated five feet in the air. Hammocks are not recommended for sleep walkers as that first step is a dangerous one. Whenever possible, I prefer the hammock to the ground but one must remember to bring a thermal pad for inside the bottom of the hammock because the cold air and wind penetrates the bottom of the hammock while the ground serves as an insulator for a tent on the ground.

We hung hammocks at five levels in these trees
I used a double hammock

Not only had Tim created the idea of the weekend excursion, he arranged the site reservations, ferry connections and confirmation of participants. I was tasked with: selection of, pre-preparation, freezing, transport and final cooking on-site for nine meals. An important consideration was that we did not have an icebox onsite and were required to haul in all our provisions as well as carry out all of our trash. That plan required careful selection, advanced preparation plus packaging and freezing of most of the perishable meals.

Because of the severe elevation changes of our daily hikes (morning noon and night) up and down the hills, our treks were somewhat extreme; at least for me at twice their age. Since I was sixty years old at the time and all of them barley crossing the thirty-year threshold, on the long daily hikes I chose to start fifteen to twenty minutes in advance of 'the kids' and allowed them to catch me forty-five minutes into the daily adventure. We started at sea level and our only choice was to hike sharply up hills to reach the first summit that rested at 2,000 feet above, before venturing off on the various trails leading to the interior of and across the island to the other beach areas. In fact, on one hike, Dan Waters carried his surfboard up and across the island to the one location where it was rumored to be viable serf. Needless to say, we burned more calories than 'a normal walk in Central Park.'

Just me and the ladies: Chanti, Dawn, Shavili & Marianne
Tim and Noah in the background.
Dan, Mike, Iram and Dominic were down the path

I spent two weeks preparing and loading my hotel room freezer with nine meals to feed eleven people and strategically loaded everything into two large roller coolers the morning of our departure. I had purchased extra-large coolers with handles and large wheels to haul the food into the campground. The plan was to keep the meals frozen as long as possible and thaw in the order of use. Thy were flattened and compressed in double

Ziploc bags, frozen solid for two weeks and tightly packed to encourage as slow a thaw cycle as possible. The nine-meal menu was selected and packed considering the defrost expectation of the food packages. Every attempt to ensure the longest thaw selections would be the latter items on the menu was a puzzle and a challenge in itself. Consideration for hard frozen versus soft-frozen was a priority. There was no room for ice therefore I had to depend on the frozen food itself keeping everything fresh for four days. Now I understand why the standard diet on a wagon-trail excursion across the United States three hundred years ago consisted of dried beans and rice and a staple of salt cured meats.

I chose the menu, shopped for the ingredients and began preparing the staples for the trip. I had to keep in mind the only storage available on the island were the bear boxes provided and the coolers we rolled to the camp site. Lunch was easy since we would be hiking most of the day and away from our campsite. We chose to take power bars plus dried fruits and nuts for lunch.

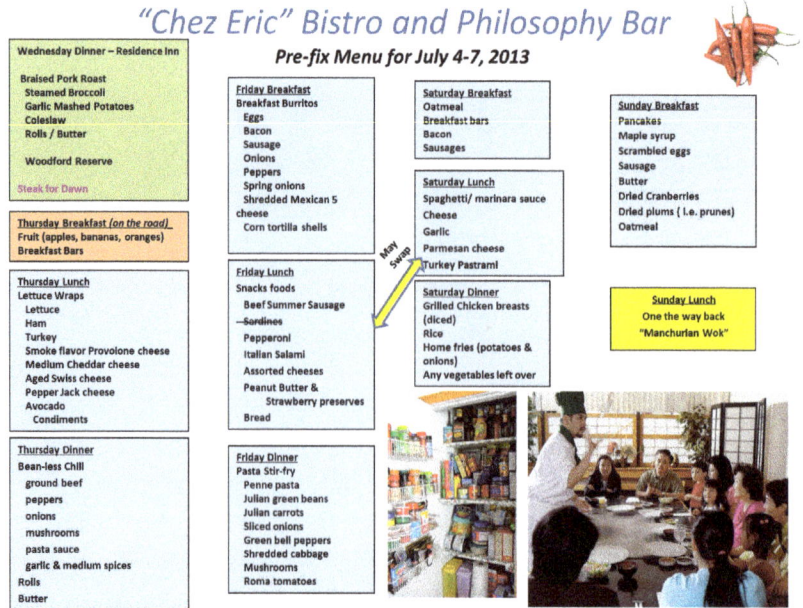

"Chez Eric" Bistro and Philosophy Bar

Pre-fix Menu for July 4-7, 2013

Wednesday Dinner – Residence Inn
Braised Pork Roast
Steamed Broccoli
Garlic Mashed Potatoes
Coleslaw
Rolls / Butter

Woodford Reserve

Steak for Dawn

Thursday Breakfast (on the road)
Fruit (apples, bananas, oranges)
Breakfast Bars

Thursday Lunch
Lettuce Wraps
Lettuce
Ham
Turkey
Smoke flavor Provolone cheese
Medium Cheddar cheese
Aged Swiss cheese
Pepper Jack cheese
Avocado
Condiments

Thursday Dinner
Bean-less Chili
ground beef
peppers
onions
mushrooms
pasta sauce
garlic & medium spices
Rolls
Butter

Friday Breakfast
Breakfast Burritos
Eggs
Bacon
Sausage
Onions
Peppers
Spring onions
Shredded Mexican 5 cheese
Corn tortilla shells

Friday Lunch
Snacks foods
Beef Summer Sausage
Sardines
Pepperoni
Italian Salami
Assorted cheeses
Peanut Butter &
Strawberry preserves
Bread

Friday Dinner
Pasta Stir-fry
Penne pasta
Julian green beans
Julian carrots
Sliced onions
Green bell peppers
Shredded cabbage
Mushrooms
Roma tomatoes

Saturday Breakfast
Oatmeal
Breakfast bars
Bacon
Sausages

Saturday Lunch
Spaghetti/ marinara sauce
Cheese
Garlic
Parmesan cheese
Turkey Pastrami

May Swap

Saturday Dinner
Grilled Chicken breasts (diced)
Rice
Home fries (potatoes & onions)
Any vegetables left over

Sunday Breakfast
Pancakes
Maple syrup
Scrambled eggs
Sausage
Butter
Dried Cranberries
Dried plums (i.e. prunes)
Oatmeal

Sunday Lunch
One the way back
"Manchurian Wok"

The meals were prepared on top of one of our two picnic tables, we used a two-burner propane camping stove provided by Tim, a couple of deep-dish frying pans and two pots for boiling water I borrowed from my hotel room. I was responsible for most of the cooking while everyone else chipped in on the set-up and cleanup for the meals.

We enjoyed a fantastic adventure that long weekend on the Island and I must give acknowledgement to the weekend attendees who inspired and shared the experience with me.

The Santa Cruz Collective included: Eric Pearson (me), Mike Jones, Tim Boyd, Iram Parveen Bilal (famous Pakistani Indie movie producer), Dawn Miller, Noah Miller, Chanti Fritzsching Waters, Dan Waters, Dominic Chi and Shivali Bidaiah. Chanti and Dan brought a hanging shower system, several boxes of wine and Dan's guitar for shared enjoyment. We experienced the luxury of running water (cold only) and bathroom facilities. However, nothing else on the island resembled 'the comforts of home'.

Three weeks to plan, prepare, freeze and store
meals plus gather all of the cooking supplies

Dan Waters on guitar & slinging his surfboard
Revernbation.com/danwaters – Los Osos, CA

Not only did Dan bring his guitar, he hauled in his surfboard and several boxes of wine which he readily shard during and after the evening meals. He also serenaded us with his songs and stories. Dan was the Site and Facilities Director for Camp Ocean Pines where we had hosted several of our Northrop Grumman Weekend Leadership Summits. We became great friends with Dan and his wife Chanti and continued to stay in touch and camped together after I changed corporate responsibilities. Honestly earned friends remain friends for life. I had learned through my journeys that true friends take you as you are and eventually become family; good or bad times, it's all the same.

We shared a lot of stories around the picnic tables as we ate our meals and bonded through our physical activities of hiking the steep hills and walking the rim of the cliffs at night while admiring the stars through the clear skies.

We found an active bat cave, but there was no sign of Batman or Robin

The numerous hills we climbed were long and steep, hence we ate and slept well from the near exhaustive journeys

A Working Dinner –
Let's Make a Deal where everybody wins

The Northrop Grumman corporate office scheduled a high-level cooperative meeting between the Senior Directors of our Radar Division out of Baltimore, Maryland and the Senior Directors of the Aerospace Division in El Segundo, California on a critical project I had been selected to serve as the 'point person' in El Segundo, California.

Five other Senior Directors of our Electronics Division flew out to Los Angeles to join us in the discussions as they represented the technical design community responsible for radar development. We met for dinner in Redondo Beach the first night they arrived. We gathered at a decent Mexican Restaurant and ordered drinks and dinner. The restaurant was noisy but pleasant, the tables and chairs were uncomfortable and the entire process seem to take forever before we received our meal. At the conclusion of dinner one of the other guys mentioned how tired he was and that these trips were such a pain having to sit two hours at the end of the day to eat dinner.

I sensed an opportunity and offered to host the crew the following evening at my place. I shared that the room was small, however I had a couch, a table and four chairs. Though it was perhaps a bit cramped, I felt I could provide a significant meal that would offer a more comfortable environment to eat dinner and discuss the business of the day. Everybody accepted and I suddenly had to plan and prepare a dinner for the six of us and two more of our on-site members working the major program we supported.

Since I generally chopped, sliced, diced and marinated my meats each weekend in preparation for the following week, I was already in good shape for their arrival the following evening. I happened to have a ten-pound pork butt (the shoulder) marinating in the refrigerator, had broccoli crowns, a head of cabbage in the refrigerator and fresh rolls on the counter. I decided it shouldn't take long to pull a dinner together. I offered Carolina Pulled Pork Barbeque (BBQ) for dinner and solicited the level of "heat" my guests could handle. Carolina BBQ is a vinegar-based recipe for pulled-pork spiced with red pepper flakes. Choosing different levels of heat produced from a variety of peppers can vary the taste with some minor variations and use of different sauces. We settled on a mild selection yet a couple of guys wanted to try my homemade hot sauce.

They asked what they could bring and I shared that although my fridge and pantry were full, I didn't have any beer, wine or spirits to share. They offered to solve that problem.

I prepared Kentucky Fried Chicken style coleslaw, from the Colonel's own recipe the night before they arrived and let it rest for twenty-four hours. I placed the marinated pork shoulder in the oven inside a large roaster at 225 degrees at 6:00 A.M. the morning of the dinner. We attended meetings all day and I went back to my hotel at 4:00 P.M. to complete the dinner preparations for their arrival at 6:00 P.M. I accomplished the breakdown of the pork, developed the sauces and cooked rice to go with the meal. I prepared three levels of heat for the BBQ sauces then pulled the pork, mixing it carefully with leftover juices and red pepper flakes. My guests were to add their own sauce choices depending on the level of heat each wanted to mix into their plate of BBQ.

My guests arrived at 6:00 P.M. as scheduled, with three bottles of wine, two six packs of a local beer, and a bottle of 15-year-old Glenlivet - single Malt Scotch. Needless to say, we didn't run out of refreshments. I also provided a gallon of sweet tea; a necessary addition when you eat great Southern BBQ. I had used my daily Per Diem (daily meal allowance) to purchase the dinner selections and my guests had used a small portion of theirs for our liquid refreshments. What a deal for all of us. We had great discussions, a relatively quick homemade delicious meal and avoided having to pay twenty percent gratuity on top of the cost of a meal out. They even left me the unopened bottle of whiskey as a gift since we had consumed the beer and wine during dinner and the after-dinner conversations.

Sweets for my Sweet

Kathy loves Savana River Pralines though she prefers they be store-bought rather than homemade. Not that they taste different, rather that these kinds of items are to be store bought, not home cooked. I finally learned this expectation over the years. However, I decided during my culinary journey in Southern California and my pursuit of becoming a contestant on Chopped, I needed to perfect at least a few baking techniques. This was my first experiment making pralines. Simple enough recipe, however the management of temperature of the cooking sugars and proper integration of the sugar and roasted pecans into the mixture before dropping on parchment paper was a challenge. Not to mention, one is dealing with hot, hot, hot liquid. Do not spill boiling sugar on your skin.

Simple Praline Ingredients: Pecans, White Sugar, Brown Sugar, Whole Milk, Vanilla Extract

Homemade Pecan Pralines
Sugar, butter and nuts offer a delightful dessert

Stuffed Cabbage for my Irish Friends – Not your Mother's Corned Beef & Cabbage dinner

Warning, this is not your traditional Corned Beef and Cabbage recipe. I had four customer visitors from out of town come to EL Segundo, who all claimed to be of Irish ancestry, though their flaming red hair might have been a dead give-away. They had been apprised of my cooking skills and offered me a deal. If I would make then a dinner consisting of corned beef and cabbage, they would provide their favorite Irish whiskey and stories of 'the old country' to spice up the meal. I suggested a variation of their request since corned beef wasn't in season, which caused a few raised eyebrows, however they were game and said in a deep Irish brogue, "We'll drink to that"!

Before we get into the meal preparation let's first school ourselves on the difference between Iris and American whiskey; one of my favorite discussions (whiskey or bourbon). It is easier than one might think. The main difference between the two whiskeys is their primary ingredients. Irish whiskey begins with barley while American whiskey can be corn, rye, or wheat. When it comes to taste, the Irish whiskey offers a lighter and less sweet flavor than the full-bodied version of the American whiskey. There you have it in a nut shell or casket as the preferred method to age the brew.

Rather than follow a simple recipe for corned beef and cabbage where you add: potatoes, carrots, celery and cabbage to create a one-pot, one step slow cooked dinner, I devised a combination of items I had in the refrigerator with the hope the blends of ingredients and flavors would satisfy my dinner guests. This was taking an unnatural chance because I seldom created a new dish for guests that I hadn't already evaluated a few times in private.

My menu preparation unexpectedly became a one pot meal. However, it involved multiple steps in preparation and cooking and it did not include corned beef. Definitely, not as easy as I had planned it to be. I chose to stuff the cabbage leaves with a Hispanic influence I had picked in El Segundo. Instead of corned beef, I substituted sliced roasted chicken I had previously cooked in the oven by roasting with several Mexican spices and injected with a liberal amount of sriracha sauce. It was flavorful and mildly spicy, though not too much heat in consideration of the average palate.

Boiled Cabbage – El dente, (just a bit of a crunch)

I started with two whole cabbages, removed the exterior leaves, cored the center and placed the entire cabbage in a large pot of boiling water until the leaves became soft and the layers began to separate. The next step was to remove and drain the cabbage while the leaves were still firm after letting them cool just enough to be able to handle them. I then carefully separated the layers.

Ingredients   *Stuffing shells*   *Crockpot cooking*

After separating the cabbage leaves, removing any hard crusts I carefully placed the leaves aside. I then began preparing the stuffing and sauce. I started with a basic marinara style sauce from the grocery store and while it simmered, I added: oregano, Italian seasoning, fresh rushed garlic cloves, fresh ground black pepper and some caramelized onions. I next added two table-spoons of paprika to provide the hint of a smoky flavor to the sauce. The dish quickly imitated a chicken enchilada casserole, except I used cabbage leaves instead of traditional soft torti-lla shells. This combination offered a low carbohydrate meal because there are only 3-5 carbs in an entire cup of cabbage.

The stuffing included: shredded roasted chicken, caramel-ized onions, grilled Anaheim, jalapeño, and red bell peppers. The ingredients were folded together and placed in the center of the larger of the cabbage leaves, then rolled tight to encase the filling.

The next step required the stuffed cabbage shells to be care-fully placed in the bottom of a slow cooker/crockpot that has been preheated on low with a small layer of marinara sauce on the bottom. I continued wrapping the combination and placed them tightly in a single layer in pot. Once the layer was full, I poured a half inch layer of the prepared sauce over the cab-bage rolls and topped with a mixture of finely shredded cheddar cheese.

Next, I proceeded with a second layer of cabbage rolls until I had exhausted the ingredients and then covered the second stuffed cabbage layer with one final layer of pasta sauce, topped with shredded cheddar cheese and a top layer of generous pizza blend cheese.

The final step was to cover the pot tightly and allowed it to continue to cook on low for six hours. I served the stuffed cab-bage using a large ladle and added additional sauce as desired.

Variety Is the Spice of Life – Baked Chicken Stuffed Cabbage

I spent one weekend experimenting with cooking techniques to develop an easier method to stuff cabbage and cook quicker that in a crockpot. I tried several different recipes and cooking methods. I discovered it was possible to prepare a mildly seasoned chicken stuffed cabbage by creating the stuffed rolls and baking them in the oven at 350 degrees for an hour and fifteen minutes. I added freshly shredded Parmesan cheese and cilantro just prior to serving.

Chicken & Cheese Stuffed Cabbage with a Cilantro garnish

Cabbage by any other name – Coleslaw is the game

Not all cabbage is cooked, and there are several varieties of cabbage used in both salads and slaws. I do not recommend using ornamental cabbage as it is not one of your garden variety cabbages intended for the dinner table. My favorite and therefore most often use of cabbage is to prepare coleslaw which only uses raw ingredients allowing one to skip the cooking process altogether. Coleslaw is a necessity whenever I prepare Carolina pulled pork barbeque (BBQ) or the Colonel's famous Kentucky fried chicken recipe.

This recipe requires one to slice and dice cabbage, carrots and onions (some people skip the onion). Finely chop the cabbage, onions and carrots, mix the raw ingredients together and fold in vinegar, sugar, salt, pepper, mayonnaise and poppy seeds. For the best results it is recommended to cover the coleslaw and set it in the refrigerator overnight. This allows the sugar to breakdown the cabbage. It softens the slaw and removes the natural bitter taste of the cabbage. There will be a runny residue of water in the bottom of the bowl that should be drained before plating and serving the coleslaw.

If you are in a pinch, you can serve coleslaw after resting in the refrigerator for two to four hours.

10 pounds of Coleslaw to accompany
30 lbs. of Carolina Pulled Pork BBQ

Mama Mia – That's a Spicy Meatball

Since my mom was mostly Italian with a dash of German heritage, I am obligated to mention Italian foods. We were introduced to spaghetti with meat sauce and meatless lasagna at a very young age. Not only was it a staple in my mom's diet growing up, it had trained her to become an expert at preparation from scratch, and it was a relatively inexpensive meal to prepare. Two pounds of hamburger was 60 cents, a pound of spaghetti 15 cents, and a loaf of Italian bread used to make garlic bread was 10 cents. A meal for five of us only cost about a dollar once mom added the tomato sauce, crushed garlic, oregano and Italian spices. Of course, at these prices I'm talking about back in the 1950's.

Weekend Retreats to Ocean Pines, Cambria, California

During my ten years leading the Northrop Grumman Recent Graduate Leadership Training Program (LTP), we held twice a year rustic, offsite four-day, and three-night experiential summit leadership weekends for 85 to 100 employees from locations across the country. During April of each year, we would congregate at Camp Round Meadow on the Coaction Mountain in Thurmont, Maryland. In September during the last four years of the program, we gathered at Camp Ocean Pines in Cambria, California. After the conclusion of the ten-year run leading the program and my transition to a corporate assignment some of us continued to drive four hours up the coast of California to spend weekends at Camp Ocean Pines.

One of the participants in the program was Tim Boyd. He was a Texas boy who played baseball and attended Caltech, where he studied Electrical Engineering. He and I would often drive up to Camp Ocean Pines on Friday evening to perform volunteer services around the camp in exchange for use of the grounds to hang our hammocks, throughout most of the year. We would occasionally use one of the rustic cabins during colder periods. We spent many nights swinging in the breeze while listening to the constant bellowing of the harbor seals who lived on and around a rock outcropping that existed just off the beach, within a couple of hundred of yards from the beach that our hammocks overlooked.

We cooked two meals a day when we camped; usually breakfast and dinner. One of my favorite meals began as an experiment when we baked a whole chicken that we cooked by assembling several large flat stones in a fire ring and constructed a make-shift oven assembled over the burning wood. We had created a stone oven, including a chimney to direct the heat and smoke up over the chicken and out the back. In addition to baking the chicken we heated soft corn and flour tortilla shells on the hot flat stones.

We prepared a rice and bean dish in a pot and made gravy from the chicken drippings.

For breakfast we used our pots and pans to prepare scrambled eggs, bacon, pancakes, biscuits, fried potatoes, oatmeal and hot cocoa. No matter how much we hiked and exercised, Tim and I always seemed to gain weight on our trips into the wilderness.

Our camping adventures extended across the country into the wilderness from Twentynine Palms (also known as 29 Palms) at the entrance to the Joshua Tree National Park. We often hiked deep into the desert and also to the Adirondack's in upper State New York where a group of us canoed and kayaked for four days and nights along flowing rivers. We enjoyed making plans, organizing attendees and preparing food for these trips. These adventures offered us an escape from the daily grind. They allowed us to clear our minds, have deep conversations about many topics and stretched our survival skills. Success depended on what we carried with us on our adventures and how we shared responsibilities.

On one of our weekend trips to Joshua Tree National Park, Tim and I ventured deep into the outback, had a great hike in sixty-degree temperatures and camped in a ravine beside a dry stream bed. There were no trees large enough for us to hang our hammocks so we pitched a two-man tent. We went to sleep around midnight after eating dinner and spending time listening to the wildlife and searching the stars. To our surprise, when we woke the following morning, the temperature had dropped to twenty degrees and it had snowed two inches. No, we had not packed any cold weather gear.

Backcountry camping at Joshua Tree with Tim Boyd
Sustained by preparing home-made beef jerky

In preparation for this trip, I had decided it was time to experiment in the kitchen with some nutritional foods and chose two selections: fruit rollups and beef jerky. Let's discuss the beef jerky because it requires bit more preparation than the fruit concoction; though both are great energy supplements and pack light if you are hiking into a wilderness situation.

Tim and I spent a lot of our free time over a five-year period finding places to hike camp and explore. I spent more time camping and learning about wilderness with him then I had done as a child in the Boy Scouts. After I returned to my hometown of Ellicott City, Maryland and retired, Tim received an assignment as a Systems Engineering Associate (SEA) at one of our Washington, D.C. locations and we were able to spend a weekend together exploring the Catoctin Mountains.

Camping in the Catoctin Mountains
with Tim Boyd

We reserved a campsite close to Round Meadow in Thurmont, Maryland where we had previously led a number of Leadership Training Program Summits. The difference being that instead of 85-100 young employees and volunteer coaches sleeping in cabins of fourteen cots each, it was just the two of us hanging our hammocks between two trees. We cooked on an open fire pit and spent two days hiking trails throughout the National Park.

Since this trip was late September and we had experienced some showers, there were only a few people in the campground. We met a rugged & somewhat ragged looking man who was also sleeping in a hammock at the campsite across the path from our site; however, his hammock had a cover tarp over his to divert the rain and provide him greater protection. He was more prepared for changing weather conditions than we had planned. We offered to share our breakfast and in return he shared stories of his days serving in the Viet Nam War and how now in his seventies he traveled around the country six months a year on his Harley Davidson motorcycle, sleeping in various State and National Parks. And, we thought our hiking and camping in the wilderness was special. Here he was, a man in his early 70's living and spending time in nature with only the basics of accommodations. He was definitely a 'Freebird'.

Pizza Anyone – Made to order specialties

When we were leading the Leadership Summits close to The Presidential Retreat, Camp David in Thurmont on the Catoctin Mountains, my Office Assistant, Donna Guilfoyle and I would use the Camp Round Meadows convection ovens and created fifty made-to-order pizzas for the attendees on Saturday night. We sliced and diced ingredients for hours, created an assembly line and pushed out pizzas for two to three hours including cleanup time.

Donna G. had an apron and baseball cap made
to authenticate my chef status at pizza creations

"Where's the Beef "(Jerky that is) – Off into the Wilderness we traveled

Now I'm hungry for wilderness food so let's make beef jerky in the oven. Since I never owned a dehydrator and was living in a hotel, the oven drying method was my only choice. This I discovered was a multi-day process. If you are going to try it, don't be in a rush, you will end up with hard, fatty and tough beef jerky. You will also end up with a smelly kitchen that even I could not avoid.

The eye of the round is the most popular cut of beef to use for beef jerky so I selected a five-pound roast that was on sale for $1.69 per pound and looked as if it was less fatty than the others in the meat case, as I dug through a large selection of roasts. I could have also use other cuts of meat if they were the ones on sale: bottom round, top round, sirloin steak or flank steak (most often used fajita and Carne Asada recipes). The lower the grade of meat you choose, the greater the fat content. Contrary to expectations, fat is bad, lean is good when preparing beef jerky.

Beef Jerky cured in the oven
A long and slow process

Let's get started. If your grocer will thinly slice your meat for you, let them, it will save you time. However, if you want to achieve the full experience as a cook it's not that difficult of a skill to learn. The butcher will automatically slice your meat against the grain for you; no need to ask. During the curing and drying process, the beef will lose approximately two-third of its weight; for every pound of beef you cure, it will yield one-third of a pound of jerky. Five pounds of meat yields 1.65 pounds, in case you left your calculator at home.

The first and most critical step in the process of preparing beef jerky is to slice it thin, very thin. The thicker the cut, the longer it takes for the beef to dehydrate during the low heat, slow cure process. Thick pieces will also turn out tough and chewy, limiting the enjoyment of the home-prepared jerky. Critical step #2 - Let it dry, let it dry, and let it dry some more.

My Beefy Jerky Marinade - modify for your personal tastes:
   1/2 cup of Soy sauce
   4 tablespoons of Worchester sauce
   4 tablespoons of brown sugar (more or less depending on your preference)
   4 teaspoons of salt, 2 teaspoons of black pepper
   2 teaspoons of cayenne pepper
   I tablespoon of sesame seeds
   2 teaspoons of onion flakes
   3 teaspoons of paprika

Mix the ingredients well then pour over the beef strips in large bowl, mix well, refrigerate covered for twenty-four hours.

My process for preparing beef jerky:

1. Remove all fat from the exterior of the meat and slice ¼" thick; across the grain.

2. Marinate your meat covered in the refrigerator for twenty-four hours.

3. Place skewers lengthwise and weave through the meat then lay out on platter.

4. Turn oven on lowest temperature possible 160 – 170 degrees for ½ hour.

5. Hang skewers from top rack with aluminum foil spread across the bottom of oven.

6. Close door and leave closed for twenty-four hours (turn on the interior light if you need to peek at the progress, opening the door will drop the temperature of the oven.

7. After twenty-four hours check jerky and if satisfied remove from oven and lay out on platters or leave in a little longer, checking every half-hour.

8. Clean oven thoroughly by wiping out and then setting a two-hour clean schedule, you don't want beef marinade in your lasagna the next time you invite friends for dinner.

9. Package the properly prepared beef jerky in zip lock bags and store until use.

10. Key Instructions to remember:

11. Slice the round against the grain if you want the best results. Slicing with the grain will cause tough and chewy jerky that some people seem to prefer; not I, and I recommend not you either. Your slices should be one-quarter of an inch thick for near optimal results. Shrinkage will vary depending on your choice of meat

12. Do not slice too thick, as it takes too long to dry and becomes chewy shoe leather, not jerky.

13. Marinate twenty-four hours after slicing.

14. Make sure meat isn't bunched to avoid uneven drying.

15. Don't open oven too early it causes a severe temperature drop.

16. Clean as you go and again after you have completed process.

17. Be Proud and enjoy, 99%+ of the people you will meet will have never made their own jerky.

Fishing in the Adirondacks –
"Man cannot live on bread alone" Matthew 4:4

Tim Boyd, Noah Miller, Mike Jones and Steve Zanias joined me for three nights and four days in the Wilderness of the Adirondacks Mountains, Upstate New York. It was late September and the last weekend the Park Service allowed anyone to go out into the wilderness, so there were only a few other campers we ran into during our adventure.

We decided not to hike, but rather canoe/kayak on a thirty-nine-mile route that required we take everything we were going to need with us into the wilderness. We were also required to bring everything out with us as well and leave no mark on the environment. We slept in open campgrounds that were more like small clearings at the edge of the rivers and lakes we traversed. There were limited cooking locations at the bank of the rivers that had crudely made out-houses with deep pits for excess bodily wastes.

We had to portage the canoes (carry them above our heads) and strap on our gear on day number two. Noah rushed ahead with his gear, came back and carried my canoe for me. I had designed and constructed a two-wheel canoe carrier that didn't work because the portage terrain was too rough for the wheels and narrow axle. We climbed with our burdens on a rocky, uphill, one-and-a-half-mile trek on land. We had to bypass a dam that stood up river in our path around the lakes. We each packed our own personal meals for the three nights on the river. I planned and prepared the meal for everyone on night #1 in the campground before we started out movements inland and on the water. We left our large pots, pans and coolers in the vehicle and packed as light as we could before embarking on the water adventure. These guys were in their early 30's and me in my mid-60's at the time of this trip.

Each of us was responsible for our own meals, cooking vessels and water for the inland excursion. I chose hot coco and tea for the chilling mornings with dried fruit and power bars for breakfast. Lunch consisted of water, peanut butter crackers and granola bars. Dinner was the only hot meal of the day and I had chosen to bring dehydrated meats, rice and beans that I had pre-cooked and froze ahead of the trip. These required rehydrating and heating. I brought a lightweight set of fishing equipment in the hopes that I might catch a fish for dinner one night. Luckily on the third afternoon I had some time to fish instead of paddling against the current. Most of the journey was harried as the intense pace the 'kids' had chosen for us was grueling.

Just in case I was going to have time to fish, I had purchased an out-of-state one-week fishing license, so my casting and potential catch would be legal. As we approached our camping area, I tossed my "Hook, Line, and Sinker", with a common earthworm attached. Ten casts into the flowing current I hooked and landed a twenty-two-inch pike. I scaled the fish, slit the belly, cleaned out the guts, added salt and pepper and a package of Italian dressing. I then double-wrapped the pike with the head attached in aluminum foil and set it in the embers of the fire for fifteen minutes. I shared the meal with the guys who were unable to catch their own fish. It was the only fish caught on the trip. Give a man a fish and he will feed a crew of five; a few bites each.

At the end of this male-bonding adventure I wrote a poem describing my personal experiences of the four nights in the wilderness with the four young men half my age.

Adventure in the Adirondacks
By Eric Paul Pearson

Five guys, four days three canoes and a kayak on the lakes and rivers in the Adirondacks
Will we make the trek with excitement and discovery without breaking our backs?

The trip began with a ten-hour, five-hundred mile drive up the back roads to nowhere

With great anticipation we made our journey while discussing how we would share

Day one ended with baked/BBQ chicken with beans and rice in the dark on an open flame
A goal to arrive pre-dusk; but the journey was slowed by unplanned changes in the lane

Day two was exciting as we entered the lake with great anticipation of the 39 miles ahead
We encountered head-winds and challenging strokes, tipped a canoe and found a lean-too

Another late dinner due to slow progress on the river; set up camp in the dark was nothing new
At night we experienced sounds of the wilderness; loons, deer, geese and an owl

Hung a bear bag to protect our food high in a tree, though Bob hadn't seen one in 15 years
No bears, no foxes, no coyotes, no deer, the night was calm as we slept under skies so clear

Late start on day three as a few took a tad too long to organize their gear
We faced a long path ahead that include porting the canoes over a mile on a path not so clear

A break on the shore offered us lunch, a deserved rest and time to fish for dinner
Lunch was quick and a nap for some, no luck for dinner as fishing was not a winner

The river was calm and the view amazing as we paddled around the bends and curves

We tried trolling for pike and trout we could see swimming under the canoes and trees

A brief stop to check the maps and agree where to pull in for the night was a smart play
We had a plan to pushed forward chatting away; we knew how far to the end of the day

We pulled into camp and began to stow our gear, time to retrieve the line & fish from the shore
Three tugs and a pull, suddenly we had a fish on the line, a pike for dinner was caught by 4:00

The last leg was a loop back towards shore with a few of us wanting far more
This old man though was glad to be back and I'm sure I wasn't the only one who was sore

One last race on the way back to the dock was more of a challenge than we had expected it to be
Not only was it against the current it ended up as another flipped canoe and a dunking for me

The "Ayes" Have it – Cooking for the Board

One element of my responsibility as the Director of new graduate recruiting and development was to represent the Northrop Grumman Corporation on several University Relations Boards. These boards consisted of Corporate Directors who facilitated the University Dean of Engineering initiatives. Over a period of six years beginning in 2006, I served first as a volunteer on committees then ascended to the position of President of The Southern Association of Colleges and Employers (SoACE). When it became my year to serve as President of the Association our Board of Directors, we attended a three-day board session and site-survey to Savanna, Georgia.

Once a year the President would hold the Semi-annual Board of Director's meeting in or around their home location. During my rein I arranged our Spring Board meeting to be in Baltimore, Maryland. I hosted one night at The Wine Bar in Fells Point and for the second night invited everyone to my home for dinner and discussions. I found it far more relaxing to have a meal and uninterrupted discussion at home. It afforded us the opportunity to arrive casually, linger around the kitchen while I finished preparing the meal and eliminated the loud noise and disturbances that occur out in a restaurant. Besides, I love to cook and show off my talents both in the kitchen and on the grill.

Since I lived in Ellicott City, Maryland at the time, just a few short miles from the Chesapeake Bay, it was necessary that as part of the meal we provide some of the world-famous Maryland steamed crabs. I was able to purchase a bushel of live jumbo crabs for $225 and then steamed the crabs on our deck as the heavy-appetizer course. We had all the necessary tools of the trade for steamed crabs: mallets, butcher paper, newspaper, trash bowls, small bowels of drawn butter, picks for the claw meat and lots of paper towels. A must have, was a sufficient supply of a local beer to wash down the crabs that were steamed live in beer and seasoned with sea salt and an overly generous amount of Maryland famous, Old Bay Seasoning.

Most of the Board members were from the Deep South and also stretched as far West as Oklahoma and Texas. The first course of Maryland Blue crabs became a lesson in picking and eating the steamed crabs. I had to demonstrate how to pull the apron, remove the top shell and expose the insides of the crab. They learned how to clean the lungs, devil and mustard away from the cherished meat. Then I demonstrated how to use the mallet to gently crush the shell on the legs and claws to remove the meat with the sharp nut picks. Once the meat was removed, they dipped the crab meat in the drawn butter, or not, and devoured the crab. There were approximately six to seven dozen crabs in that size in a bushel.

In my past history, when there were extra steamed crabs, I would pick the meat, freeze it, and at a future date prepared Maryland crab cakes with a light breading of crushed crackers, mayonnaise, butter, eggs and additional Old Bay seasoning. I took the carefully blended ingredients (did not over stir) and formed a lightly packed ball. I dropped the softball sized crab balls in the deep fryer for a couple of minutes or smashed them down and cooked them a few minutes under the broiler in the oven. Making crab cakes created one of the best uses of leftovers a chef could offer.

While my guests spent the next hour picking and eating crabs while washing down the spices with beer and wine, I prepared the second course on the grill. Half of the board was from beef country so I made the bold choice to prepare prime rib and porterhouse steaks on the grill, along with sweet corn on the cob and rather large loaded double-stuffed baked potatoes. My goal was to make them feel like they were eating at Ruth's Chris Steak House.

Perfect prime rib can be a difficult task to achieve, and disappointing if you overcook the roast, especially if people are watching you and want to peek at the progress. The perfect prime rib requires maintaining a constant temperature. The backyard chef must leave the grill covered until he feels the meat is at optimum temperature, remembering it must rest after removing from the grill to avoid all the juices leaking out causing the meat to become dry and chewy. It is often difficult to find bone-in prime rib in the grocery store and any great chef will share the importance of grilling with the bone on. Prime rib should not be cooked directly on the grill. Elevate the prime rib over an oven safe bowl of beef broth and setting it on a rack during the cooking process. Let it cook approximately thirty-five minutes per pound at two-hundred-twenty-five degrees until internal temperature reaches one-hundred-ten degrees. Let the roast sit thirty minutes and then sear it for fifteen minutes prior to slicing and serving.

Prime Rib on the grill with mashed potatoes, gravy and sautéed mushrooms

The porterhouse steaks also have a critical period after reaching the proper temperature that they must sit off the flame and 'rest' to ensure the juices spread out in the steak and don't bleed on your plate rendering a great piece of beef to become tough and chewy. Grill the steak five minutes on each side, rotating 90 degrees after two minutes to create the grill marks on the outside. It will also ensure the steak cooks from the inside out rather than outside in and it's better to undercook than over cook. Never let the steak reach higher than 145 degrees.

3" thick porterhouse steak twice baked potatoes
Fresh steamed green beans with sliced bell peppers,
caramelized onions and mushrooms

The corn, broccoli crowns and potatoes are easy to prepare, so they are barely mentioned here. I also prepared a mixed salad for those who weren't interested in either steamed crabs or porterhouse steaks. Let it be said that the rabbits enjoyed the leftover salad during the following week.

"I've Been Chopped" –
A sad yet exhilarating experience

Failure is not the results of being beaten by a more formidable opponent; rather failure is having not tried in the first place. One cannot improve his or her talents in the kitchen and become a welcomed host without facing the odds of failure and the ultimate success gained from repetitive trials and incremental improvements. Hasn't everyone at least once burned the family dinner during a holiday season event? Or, perhaps left the meat in the oven too long and it became the consistency of a hockey puck. Better yet, who of us have never forgotten to thaw the turkey before Thanksgiving dinner?

When my father-in-law, Herman Leroy Brackett would make a mistake with a meal and was chided by one of his daughters, his response was always the same, "But, that's just how I like it." He proceeded to eat the unrecognizable dish as if had been prepared in the manner it was intended, including the day he used liquid soap instead of vegetable oil.

Everybody's grandmother has a special recipe that was handed down generation to generation. Most included the incorporation of lard (you might have to look this word up). My fear is that with the growth of meal packages delivered to your door and prepared in under thirty minutes will cause Grandmother's favorites to be lost forever. History will be rewritten.

Near the conclusion of my adventure with cooking on the road as I completed my assignment in California, I noticed that the Food Channel was soliciting applicants for the series of Chopped television series and there was one for novice cooks. After years of passion for cooking and three short years of modeling the Chopped Kitchen in my hotel room, I felt I was ready for the challenge. The thought of me even getting to the first step of interviews would be an accomplishment. Therefore, I carefully read the application criteria and began to complete my personal history of cooking expertise, reviewed my submission, carefully checked for content and spelling errors and released my application. I had boldly applied for Chopped under the category of Non-Professionals.

Months went by since I had filed my application and I had given up on being considered for Chopped as candidate for participation. I had all but forgotten I had applied, yet the hope was always in the back of my mind and I often dreamed of the possibility. I had not shared with anyone of my application because I assumed this was probably one of the greatest stretch attempts, I had made in my life. I did not wish to advertise an impending failure.

One day shortly after retirement from Northrop Grumman and moving back to Maryland during the fall of 2014, upon checking my email I noticed I had received an email from "Chopped Casting." The excitement of an email alone sent my hopes sky high and my heart rate quickly doubled. The email notified me of their interest in my application and requested my response to continued interest in interviewing for Chopped for Grandparents. I did not know that was a category on Chopped but I wasn't going to let the opportunity pass me by and quickly responded that I was indeed interested and excited to share my thoughts of meals I had prepared for our grandchildren over the years.

Just a few days later I received another email and an invitation to be interviewed for the show through a Skype interview. As they say in the horse business, "we were off to the races." I accepted the date and time, downloaded Skype on my computer and set up my desk in our family room providing the best background I could for this all important, one-shot attempt to impress the participant selection team. Was I nervous? You bet I was, with a chance of a lifetime hinging on a twenty-minute interview over the computer. I felt the interview went well. I was confident yet a bit nervous and comfortable with most of the questions that were asked. My only reservation was when I was asked what my future plans were if I was selected, participated and won Chopped for Grandfathers. I honestly replied that I wasn't interested in becoming a professional chef and was concerned that might be the wrong answer, though I had to be honest with myself.

After waiting another six weeks I received a third email from Chopped Casting. It started out with a thank you, BUT ... "we have selected other more qualified grandparents to compete and suggest you keep watching for other potential opportunities." At least I had made it to the personal interview stage and was a finalist for consideration. However, as they say in the carnival industry, "Close but no cigar."

Since that devastating, cold day in December of 2014, I applied for Chopped three more times, the most recently having been January 16, 2019. At the time of this writing, I had received two, "thanks but no thanks, keep trying" and will continue beefing up my culinary resume application in hopes of that one opportunity to pursue a life-long dream.

Deep-Fried Bacon Cheeseburger Recipe – You will think you are in Heaven

As Wimpy in the Popeye cartoons always said, "I'll gladly pay you Tuesday for a hamburger today," who doesn't love cheeseburgers, bacon, or deep-fried foods? I decided why not put all three elements together and create a one-time 1,000 (well, maybe 2,000) calorie man-size meal. There is a limit to the amount of grease and calories one can maintain in their diet and as most of my dishes are selected and created with lean thoughts. We all must have one or two crutches in our lives. I love burgers and yes, I know there are a lot less calories in a turkey burger than a hamburger, therefore I restrict myself to one cheeseburger per month. It can be out in public or in the privacy of my home away from home, but one is my limit. The deep-fried bacon cheeseburger might be a bit overboard, yet it does exist in my inventory of main dishes. I created this one on a dare to see if it could be done and believe me, it's worth every single calorie included in this greasy and delicious entree.

Having not calculated the actual caloric measurement, this recipe may very well be a 2,000-calorie excessive selection, but who doesn't deserve it once a month? Add fries with the order as recommended below and you just might reach a 2,500 calorie, one course meal. And we aren't event mentioning a milkshake to wash it all down.

Deep Fried Bacon Cheeseburger Ingredients:
    1 lb. 90/10 fresh ground beef (lean)
    1 lb. thick cut smoked maple bacon
    8 oz. chunk sharp cheddar cheese
    4 oz. thin sliced mozzarella cheese
    Salt & pepper to taste (some people chose to use Seasoned Salt or Steak seasonings)

The Maturation Process of the Deep-Fried Bacon Cheeseburger
A burger worth waiting for

1. Season the ground beef with salt, pepper and any other spice you choose and mix thoroughly (not too many though)
2. Flatten ground beef out to approximately 1/2" thick in a rectangular shape
3. Place sharp cheddar cheese in center of ground beef and fold ground beef to completely encase cheese by sealing the edges of the patty
4. Cut 1lb. package of thick cut maple bacon in half and create two lattices of bacon (as shown above)
5. Wrap ground beef and cheese in bacon, press to adhere bacon to ground beef and secure edges
6. Secure bacon to the ground beef with toothpick (remember to remove toothpicks after cooking)

7. Carefully place burger in pot of oil at 370 to 400 degrees for 3-4 minutes, roll over and cook an additional 3-4 minutes until bacon is crisp

8. Remove bacon cheeseburger from oil, drain and pat dry with paper towel

9. Choose your favorite bread/roll, add lettuce, tomato, mayonnaise, ketchup and mustard (as you prefer) and enjoy alongside the two-step French fries explained below. Enjoy, burp once or twice and prepare to take a restful nap. Don't forget to wipe the catsup and mustard off your cheeks, your shirt and your lap.

French Fried Potatoes Done Right – The two-step process to achieve perfection

Once you have accepted the challenge and have taken the plunge to create your Mega Deep Fried Bacon Cheeseburger you can't stop there. You already have the pot of hot cooking oil so why not add the perfect All American French fries to the plate?

It is not as simple as grabbing a bag of potatoes, peeling and slicing them, dumping them in a deep fryer and pulling them out at a preselected time. There are a couple of methods to create the perfect addition to your Deep-Fried Bacon Cheeseburger. They involve careful selection of potatoes and the adoption of a proven cooking process. One must be careful to avoid rushing the process or you will end up with uncooked and/or soggy fries inside with a deceivingly and appealing browned crisp exterior.

1. Choose the right potatoes first; I recommend 4-5 Russet potatoes though others suggest Yukon Gold.
2. Choose your favorite oil; Canola, Peanut, lard
3. Wash potatoes under cold water and remove any spots with a paring knife
4. Peel the potatoes on the sides leaving the skin on the ends
5. Slice potatoes lengthwise about 1/8" thick and again to create 1/8" by 1/8" potatoes
6. Soak in cold water twenty minutes (up to twenty-four hours) to remove excess starch.
7. Drain and dry potatoes to remove excess water
8. Cook small amounts of potatoes at a time for 6 to 7 minutes at 320 degrees; drain and dry
9. Raise temperature of oil to 350 degrees, place a moderate number of potatoes in oil and cook 2-3 minutes until golden brown
10. Drain potatoes and salt while they are hot

11. Make sure oil temperature has recovered and continue cooking fries until complete

12. Enjoy with your Deep-Fried Bacon Cheeseburger and favorite condiments

Nutrition Facts
Calories in Homemade French
Fries (1 potato)
Serving Size: 1 serving
Amount Per Serving
Calories 118.0
Total Fat 0.0 g
Saturated Fat 0.0 g
Polyunsaturated Fat 0.0 g
Monounsaturated Fat 0.0 g
Cholesterol 0.0 mg
Sodium 5.0 mg
Potassium 515.0 mg
Total Carbohydrate 27.0 g
Dietary Fiber 2.0 g
Sugars 1.0 g
Protein 2.0 g
Vitamin A
Carbohydeates 25 g

If you and your family eat a lot of French fries and would like to save on prep time as well as kitchen clean-up, you can peel and cut large amounts of fries, complete the precook cycle at 320 degrees, drain and then freeze the potatoes in serving size Ziploc® freezer bags. When ready to use the frozen fries, remove them from freezer and complete the second stage of the cooking process. When you are ready to cook the stored fries, heat the oil to 375 degrees and cook the frozen fries one and a half to two minutes. Be careful of possible splattering as any ice melting will pop in the hot oil.

One Can Never Have Enough Bacon – Pig on Pig

I cook a lot of meals with "the other white meat," pork. We love bacon, pork roasts, pork belly, pork chops, pork barbeque, pork rinds, baby back pork ribs, spiral-cut honey baked ham, and pork sausage. We don't eat pork every day and we carefully spread it out in our menu planning throughout the year.

We also worked to limit the amount of fat/grease in our diet by selecting the leaner cuts of the pig. The menu adaptations allowed us to provide cooked entrées such that we removed as much of the fat possible. We have been careful with roasts to make sure we didn't cause the meat to dry out in the process. Of course, when one prepares a Boston butt (shoulder) it is full of large sections of connective tissue and fat. Trim too much fat and you lose the natural flavors and tenderness of the entrée.

This group is offered as an example of three bacon wrapped entrees in pictures:

1. Bacon wrapped center cut pork loin
2. Bacon wrapped broiled sea scallops (dinner entrée or appetizer)
3. Bacon wrapped; cheese filled boneless chicken thighs (both white meats together)

Lattice wrap center cut boneless pork loin with think cut bacon

Loin and bacon to keep bacon in place. Brown all sides 3-4 minutes in hot bacon dripping (grease)

Cook in center of heated oven at 375 degrees until pork in 135 degrees (appx. 1.5 hours)

Remove from oven, let rest for twenty minutes and slice to desired thickness

Bacon Roses, broiled to perfection

Bacon wrapped boneless chicken thighs – By the picture's recipe

Let's try your skill at preparing a dish without the ingredients listed, just the pictures and absorb the caption descriptions to create a juicy and delicious dinner entrée. Combine with mashed potatoes or rice, gravy made from the drippings and your favorite green vegetable.

Ingredients laid out for assembly

Assembly in motion – cheese stuffed & rolled

Raked and stacked for a 350 degree oven

The "Piece de la resistance"

Bacon wrapped boneless chicken thighs
steamed rice and gravy (the rue of the day)
Dinner is served – small portions

You Can Bank on It – Staff Luncheon

From the time I retired to Elizabethtown, Kentucky and selected a local bank based in our Kroeger store I have been blessed with tremendous full-service treatment almost everywhere I went. I had discovered the bank on my first visit to the grocery store and every time I shopped at the store I stopped by and visited, chatted, and engaged in purposeful and often conversation that resulted in much laughter. Denesa was the Branch manager and made me feel at home the first day I visited the counter.

They not only handled all of our banking needs, they assisted my son in arrangements for his move from Maryland to Kentucky, transfer of documents across state lines, registration and payment of auto transfers and advice on acquiring a business loan.

Denesa (3rd from right) & her Staff

WesBanco – Elizabethtown, KY

I was always sharing my escapades of cooking and the development of this book. They became non-volunteers on my journey to *What's Cookin'*. I never stopped talking to ask, I just assumed they enjoyed the stories and appeared to have listened intently as I rattled off many of the recipes I had created and shared with others.

WesBanco had bought United Bank who had a few years before bought 1st National Bank and absorbed all of the assets. They closed the Kroeger grocery store location where I shopped and moved the staff to the existing WesBanco location a mile up the road. Denesa and her staff was transferred and she remained as the branch manager of the full-service WesBanco location. It was a traditional setup for a bank with offices and seating area as customers entered the door and a large safe in the back guarded by bars and locks.

They even had hot coffee and cookies that were unavailable at their former location in the grocery store. Although I rarely drank coffee, I would stop in for a cup of coffee as my excuse to visit the ladies in the bank. My true purpose being so that I could tell a few stories I had recently experienced.

One day, after living in Elizabethtown for three years full-time, I realized that "all talk and no action" or better yet, "actions speak louder than words" that it was time I rewarded my loyal listeners with an opportunity to evaluate and critique my culinary claims. What to make was my dilemma. It needed to be light, cool rather than hot, more than one choice and easy to store in the small refrigerator at the bank. They had a large vault for the money, but a small breakroom for the employees.

I decided chicken would be the featured entree for the luncheon. I prepared my well-known chicken salad with white meat only, mayonnaise (not salad dressing), lemon juice, salt & pepper, diced celery, a small amount of diced sweet onion, sweet pickle relish and finely a couple of chopped hard-boiled eggs. I boiled an additional dozen eggs, deconstructed them and constructed egg salad quite similar to my chicken salad recipe except it has more eggs and no chicken. I provided a gallon of sweet tea, a gallon of lemonade, a large bag of ripple cut potato chips and a container of my home-made sweet bread and butter pickles. And, there was fresh washed lettuce, one dozen crescent rolls and a dozen hard rolls, plus: plates, napkins and serving utensils.

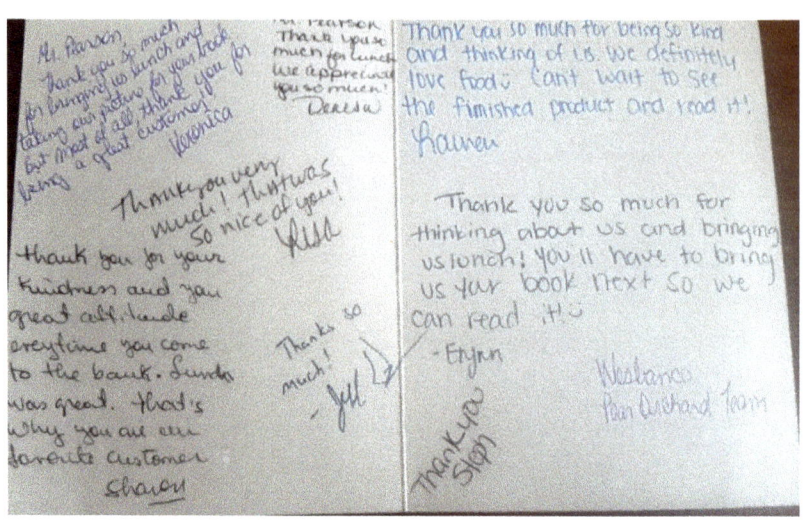

To my surprise a week after the impromptu luncheon,
I received a thank you card in the mail

The Dentist Office –
It's not always about pulling teeth

We traveled forty-five minutes south of Elizabethtown for our dental check-ups and the occasional filling beginning in 2012 when we purchased our retirement home in Elizabethtown, Kentucky. Our dentist for six years, Dr. Allen Shelton passed away suddenly of a heart attack at age sixty. Dr. Shelton was a kind and gentle man, University of Kentucky graduate and spent significant time volunteering service for the local Kentucky State prison system. He always shared stories of growing up in the country and his meager rise to becoming a revered dentist in Central Kentucky. He served the local community for over thirty-seven years before his death. He was an active person, who loved his University of Kentucky sports and playing golf. He will be missed by many.

Six months late Dr, Cadence Flener, DMD took over Dr. Shelton's practice. She is a little woman who quickly filled those big shoes. I had shared copies of my first two books with the office staff and held many discussions with the receptionist team while waiting for my time in the chair. Upon mentioning I was writing this book about food and people they demanded I provide a tasting of my cooking skills to prove my capabilities as a homeschooled chef matched my repertoire as a published author.

The next time I drove down to Mumford for my checkup and cleaning I brought my holiday inspired deviled eggs. All eggs were eaten prior to my being able to exit the door. I had hoped to be offered a free cleaning and two cavities repaired in exchange. Deviled eggs are really just another way to serve chicken, proof that the egg came before the chicken, in the instance at least.

Dr. Candace Flener (left) and her staff – special deviled eggs

Chicken Salad for the Soul –
An unexpected conversation before lunch

I spent a week doing major landscaping for my daughter and her husband as I took care of their three cats and two dogs for a week while they enjoyed their honeymoon cruise to the Bahamas. I had trimmed and culled trees, ripped out seedlings, pulled briars, raked up beds full of pine straw, and transplanted several plants from our more mature beds back home in Kentucky. Many of those plants had followed us from our home of thirty years in Maryland. The last task was to spread a truckload of mulch onto all of the flower beds and the play area in the backyard.

I had spent an hour measuring beds and calculating square feet to cubic feet to cubic yards and came up with a calculation that it would take seventeen cubic yards of hardwood mulch to cover the beds to a depth of three inches. They have odd shaped beds so I was forced to use my high school Algebra to complete the calculations. An extremely large dump truck showed up and deposited an enormous amount of black hardwood mulch on a ten foot by twenty-foot tarp I had laid out to protect the driveway and the grass. As I surveyed the mountain of triple-shredded trees before me that was piled as high as I am tall, I began to feel I had undertaken a chore too big for one person. It was like the day I tried to eat my one pound deep fried bacon wrapped cheeseburger. Too late now, it was there and had to be gone before Erika's return on Sunday.

Crepe Myrtle bed before

17 Cu. Ft. Hardwood mulch

Crepe Myrtle bed after

I labored an entire day with a pitch fork and a wheelbarrow and moved approximately one-half of the pile. I had covered six of the beds leaving me the two largest areas including the play area with the swing set in the backyard. As I started day two moving mulch my back was sore and all I wanted to do was get the job finished and level the beds. A man, who I learned was named Terry came walking down the street and offered to help me move the rest of the mulch. I declined and mumbled that it was my job for the week and I needed the exercise. Instead of walking on, Terry began talking, more like rambling, and that was when I noticed how sad his eyes were, and on the verge of tears. I began to listen more intently at that point. I realized this man had a story he needed to tell someone, anyone, everyone.

He said he was going to help the woman across the street with a leaking radiator hose. He added that he was just looking for things to do to keep busy because he was depressed that his thirty-two-year-old son had committed suicide three weeks prior. I listened patiently as Terry spoke for about twenty-five minutes before I shared some of my own pain and understanding from losing one of my own family members fifteen years previous. He headed across the street to look at the radiator and hollered back, I'll be back to help you finish your task so I followed him over to the neighbors to see if I could help as well.

I took a break for an hour and played with the dogs and then there was a knock on the door. Terry was there with a leaf blower and a pitch fork and he said, "Let's get this done, I'll do the work and you just walk and talk with me while I do it. I don't want any money; just talking to you is helping me with my pain." For the next three hours Terry carried most of the conversation and I occasionally offered encouragement and thoughts when he would stop and ask for my experiences. He loved his son dearly and they had worked together for quite some time framing houses, doing carpentry and landscaping. His missed him and wanted to know when the pain would stop. He thanked me for letting him work and talk and decided my ambition and stories had motivated him to write his own book about his own son's life as I had done with our so Ryan titled, *Ryan's Stories: God's Perfect Child.*

Terry offered some amazing life stories, lots of humor and some rather scary events that had taken place with his son. He also has interesting hobbies: he is amazing chess player, raises orchids which I have found to be next to impossible, is an excellent story teller and has always had the desire to author his one book.

I'll save for another time the story how he was attacked by a much larger man that made it necessary for Terry to pull a knife that saved his life; leaving the other man with a colostomy for the rest of his life. I do have to share that the Prosecutor offered Terry a twenty-year sentence reduced to ten on the second offering in the penitentiary and a $10,000 fine. Terry opted to go to trial and it only took two hours for the jury to come back, "innocent on all charges. Apparently, it was decided that this was a clear case of self-defense. Was the prosecutor looking for justice or just another conviction on his record? No comment, you be the judge.

As we wrapped up moving and spreading the last eight cubic yards of mulch, Terry insisted on raking the grass and blowing the shreds while I stood around watching. I offered for Terry to join me for lunch since I was going to eat a chicken salad sandwich, I had made the night before. It was fresh and light with just the right combination of mayonnaise, salad dressing, salt and pepper, chopped onions, chopped celery and sweet pickle relish. It's one of my favorite quick meals I liked to prepare. Occasionally I would also add a couple of hard-boiled eggs.

Chicken Salad for the Soul – On toast and with LTM and on a Croissant

Terry said he hadn't eaten much since his son's passing and wasn't sure he could eat but. "Thank you anyway." I insisted that he required nourishment to continue forward so he took a sandwich with him and promised he would eat it. Then he invited me to dinner at his house around the corner for later in the week. He thanked me once again, and with tears in his eyes gave me a hug and said, "You have no idea how much you helped me today and have inspired me to ensure my son's past has a purpose going forward. I want to write about his life and get all his friends to contribute their stories." In return, Terry provided me time with someone else to share efforts and stories. I believe I received as much joy out of the chance meeting as he did that day.

Be it chicken soup or chicken salad, food brings people together, and people coming together generates meaningful conversation. I was blessed that day when Terry strolled down the street and offered to help me, neither of us realizing that I was there to help him. We don't always know what to say when we speak with a stranger however, I found through the years that the more I listened and the less I talked, the message becomes clearer and I could better serve another's needs.

Two days later Terry went back to help and replace the leaking radiator hose on woman's car. I stopped over to offer my experience and said, "Yep, it's leaking all right" and showed him where the hole in the hose was and where the two clamps holding the hose in place were located. Terry invited me to dinner that night and suggested the woman we were helping would assist him by making the dinner. I could see that she wasn't too happy with the offer as she is a single mother of young boys, so I stepped in and suggested I might have a better solution and offered to make dinner for everyone. I drove to Kroger® for supplies and created a chicken noodle casserole with sides steamed broccoli and green beans. With a sigh of relief and a big smile on her face Patrice said thank you and we agreed I would have dinner ready for pickup at 6:00 p.m.

Even though I have prepared many chicken dishes over the years, I had never constructed a chicken noodle casserole. I went to the web, pulled one from my favorite site, Allrecipes.com and headed to the grocery store with my list of ingredients in hand. Having never made this kind of casserole before or cooked for these people, I followed the recipe exactly as written; avoiding any deviation though the thought crossed my mind several times. Well not exactly because I changed the quantities of soup and doubled the amount of sour cream and did not put any onion in the casserole. I guess I did modify the recipe and will have to post my recipe instead of the one I pulled from the web. I knew I needed to increase the quantities by proportion and I eliminated the onion because not everyone likes onions.

Baked Chicken Noodle Casserole

Plated Chicken Noodle Casserole dinner

Ingredients:
1 – 16 oz. can of cream of chicken soup
1 – 16 oz. can of cream of mushroom soup
2 cups of sour cream (regular is fine)
16 oz. pkg. extra-wide egg noodles
Salt to taste
Fresh ground pepper to taste
½ - Cup melted butter
1 – Cup crumbled buttery crackers
4 – Large boneless and skinless chicken breasts

Instructions:
Preheat oven on 350 degrees and set rack in center of oven
Poach the chicken breasts for 12 - 15 minutes on simmer until breasts are pink inside
Remove chicken and set aside while you raise the chicken water to boil and cook the egg noodles per instructions on the box and drain
Mix cream of chicken soup, cream of mushroom soup and sour cream together while adding salt and pepper to taste
Cut chicken breasts into bite-sized chunks and fold into sauce mixture
Carefully fold egg noodles into mixture avoiding beating chicken and noodles into small pieces
Spread noodles and chicken mixture into greased 9 by 13 casserole dish
Melt ½ cup (1 stick) of butter in sauce pan and add crumbled buttery crackers
Spread cracker/butter mixture on top of casserole
Cook in a 350-degree oven on center rack for 30 minutes until casserole is bubbly and crumble has browned
Let cool for ten minutes and serve with steamed vegetables and a light salad

As mentioned above, the standard recipe calls for one white onion chopped and caramelized and some recipes add one cup of grated cheese to the liquid mix prior to adding the chicken and noodles.

Wings & Things – Sometimes chicken doesn't taste like chicken

We eat a fair amount of chicken in or home so we found it important to prepare in a number of different ways and although everything else "tastes like chicken" we chose to spice things up and create different dishes with a variety of seasonings. The puppies prefer lots of oven baked chicken pieces with or without the skin and they are less likely to request any spicy additions to their preparation.

We have also enjoyed a regular dose of chicken salad. It is fairly easy to prepare, stores well and you can make it when you have time. It serves well when you put it away in the refrigerator to have for lunch, snacks, in a salad, as a sandwich or when the neighbors unexpectedly stop by. You can even serve it as lettuce wraps for those concerned about carbohydrates or the extra calories from bread. My wife enjoys the chicken salad on her gluten-free crackers as an evening snack.

When I had the time to plan the meals for three or four days at a time, I started by purchasing two whole chickens, on sale of course. I would butcher them by removing the wings, legs, thighs and backs, leaving four full breasts with the ribs attached. The chicken breasts were then seasoned with, pepper and seasoned salt and cooked for forty-five minutes to an hour at three-hundred-and-fifty degrees. After I cooled the breasts, I removed the rib and back bone extensions and put in the refrigerator for chicken salad.

That left the legs, thighs, and two parts of the wings to make Buffalo chicken wings with legs for me, which I would often double-dip and fry. One chicken three ways was always a nice option. When the day was full of "March Madness" college basketball games, it seemed appropriate to make oven baked wings and things.

I have done chicken legs and thighs several ways. Here are two examples,

1) triple-dipped in flour and egg and deep fried in oil to create crispy skin and 2) more simply dusted with a baking powder mixture and baked in the oven. Most of my dinner guests prefer the deep-fried solution. The lesser calorie version also provides a crispy coating while maintaining an interior full of moisture and taste.

Roasters are generally raised for three to five months and weigh 5 to 7 lbs. Because of their age they contain a thicker layer of fat that serves to baste the chicken during cooking and are best prepared at lower temperatures than broiler/fryers. The difference between broiler/fryers and roasters is typically determined by the age and size of the chicken. Broiler/Fryers go to market at about six to eight weeks and weigh three to four lbs. These chickens are younger, tenderer than roasters and are best cooked with high heat.

Here is my stove top deep-fried chicken process. I started with two whole chickens. I have done this with both broiler/frying and roasting chickens, however selecting broiler/fryers in the better solution for this application. Purchase three broiler/fryers (count the drumsticks in the picture) and butcher them, removing the backs creating eight pieces per chicken. Create a mixture of pepper, thyme, a dash of paprika and garlic powder. Coat the chicken pieces (or season to your tastes). Dredge through a milk bath and soak for three hours to overnight.

Remove the chicken from the refrigerator and allow ½ hour for the chicken to come up to room temperature. Set three medium bowls out and put flour, milk and flour or breadcrumbs in the bowls. Dry all chicken pieces with paper towels then dip them in flour, milk, the second flour and set aside until all of the chicken is coated.

Using either a deep fryer, or in my case a deep frying pan, heat your choice of oil to 350 degrees and slowly lower your chicken pieces with tongs into the oil. Do not crowd the pan or you will significantly drop the temperature of the oil creating greasy pieces.

Turn the chicken every 2-3 minutes until the outside is golden brown and the internal temperature reaches 165 degrees. It takes approximately 10 minutes for wings and 12 minutes for thighs, legs and breasts.

Drain each piece by shaking off the excess oil in the pan and then set on paper towels. Let cool 10 minutes and serve warm with your favorite vegetables (I prefer French fries or mashed potatoes with gravy and coleslaw. Add a green vegetable and salad of choice.

Deep Fried Chicken in Canola Oil at the Residence Inn®, El Segundo, California

Here is my recommended process for oven fried chicken. I washed and damp dried the chicken parts and then set them out on a pan to dry while I created the rub. To create crispy chicken in the oven was the goal and to avoid any excess oil saturating the skin when using a deep fryer. I also wanted to avoid the massive spatters that occur when cooking in a pan on the stove top.

The rub consisted of three tablespoons of Aluminum free baking powder mixed with two teaspoons of ground black pepper, two teaspoons of dried crushed garlic and a teaspoon of cayenne pepper. I did not add salt to the mixture because I had found that applying salt at this stage tends to draw the moisture out of the chicken during cooking and the smaller pieces tend to became dry and chewy.

The next step was to preheat the oven to four-twenty-five to forty-fifty degrees and put the oven rack in the middle. I then mixed the chicken pieces in the baking powder mixture and shook off the excess before placing on a cooking sheet. I lined a baking pan with aluminum foil and placed a rack in the pan with the purpose of raising the chicken off the foil. The chicken pieces were evenly spaced on the baking rack with the meatier legs in the center and placed in the oven.

I set the timer for twenty minutes, turned the chicken pieces over to facilitate an even cook and crusty skin on both sides, then returned the pan to the oven and set the timer for twenty more minutes. I pulled the wing and thigh pieces at the end of the twenty minutes and returned the legs to the oven for ten additional minutes.

Dried, dusted & ready for the oven   Cooked to perfection, ready for sauce
Oven baked Fried Chicken with Baking Flour coating

The final step was to create the desired buffalo chicken sauce. I have developed ten different sauces I like to use and they range from quite mild to almost throat burning heat with one using ghost peppers I had grown in my own garden. I recommend that even the skilled chef consider the audience and carefully decide how much heat to add to their sauce. I like to start with a jar of smoky and/or brown sugar-based sauce then add different spices and fresh or dried peppers to taste from my garden collection. One must constantly taste and adjust the sauce until satisfied. Occasionally the sauce preparation takes longer than the preparation and cooking of the Buffalo wings. Some of my peppers were dried and stored in a cool dry area to avoid mold while others were pickled and stored for long-term use in sealed mason jars.

About The Author – Eric Paul Pearson

Eric Pearson started working at age ten, performing odd jobs in the neighborhood, such as babysitting, yard work, snow shoveling, gardening. From the age twelve through sixteen he delivered newspapers once a week at 4:30 a.m. every Wednesday. "Neither Sleet nor Snow nor Rain nor Shine" ever kept the weekly paper from being delivered. That dedication and drive, combined with the experience of spending his lunch hours in elementary school alongside his sister Jeannette to assist severely disabled students, has led to a life of service and several career positions in a variety of different worlds.

Eric has always been known as a risk taker, and no opportunity or responsibility ever presented itself as too challenging. He became a swim coach, a basketball coach, and a lacrosse coach, having never played the games competitively. He became a varsity soccer player at North Carolina State University in 1967, despite the fact he had never even kicked a soccer ball before the first day of practice.

After suffering through High School with severe learning comprehension disabilities, Eric graduated Magna Cum Laude with a B.S. in Education from Bowie State University and a Dual M.S., Magna Cum Laude from Johns Hopkins University Whiting School of Engineering. He taught middle school science and coached four varsity sports, as well as the Juniors Swim Team at the United States Naval Academy. Eric's education led him to a successful thirty-year career in Radar Defense Electronics. There he ran antenna development teams and later created a nationally recognized Recent Graduate Professional Development Program (PDP) for engineers and scientists and a Leadership Training Program (LTP) for Northrop Grumman Electronic Systems that expanded across the United States for over ten years.

Throughout his careers, Eric volunteered to serve on university engineering advisory boards at North Carolina State University, served as a volunteer adjunct professor at California Polytechnic University in San Luis Obispo California for eight years, and served as a speaker, mentor, and board member for the National Association of Colleges and Employers (NACE), the Southern Association of Colleges and Employers (SoACE), the American Society for Engineering Education (ASEE), and the Cooperative and Experiential Education Division (CEED) of the ASEE.

Eric can be reached at *eric@thebottomthree.com*

Eric began his writing career in 2004 after the death of his profoundly disabled son, Ryan. Ryan was born with a minimally functioning brain and at two months began to have grand mal seizures. The medical community indicated Ryan wasn't supposed to live two years; however, he blessed the family with fourteen wonderful years of excitement and events. Upon Ryan's death on March 16, 2004, Eric began to author his first book and published the tales of Ryan's life in *Ryan's Stories: God's Perfect*

Child which he released in 2008 to share with families who had similar experiences of struggles and loss.

In 2017 Eric published his second non-fiction book about people and relationships titled, *The People You Meet in First Class: When Chance Meetings Become Life Changing Conversations.* In this book he shared how his experiences of flying over a forty-year period for mostly business that led him through his journey and interest in other people, to observe what often happens in and around airports and planes during forty years of travel. He felt that he was put in a purposeful situations and specific seats on planes to engage in courtesy conversations that often became deep interchanges, resulting in helping people navigate through their own personal turmoil. These chance meetings are shared throughout the book.

Throughout Eric's third book, *"What's Cookin': Feeding the Heart and Soul Through the Alimentary Canal"* Eric continued his journey of sharing true stories about people and relationships developed through cooking and sharing of meals. Though he can't "build a better mousetrap", he sure knows how to build a better burger.

Not Your Basic Naked Bacon Cheeseburger with
Grilled Jalapeno Peppers (750 calorie & Gluten Free)

Eric's previous book, *The People You Meet in First Class: When chance meetings become life changing conversations,* was nominated for two awards in 2018: The Author Academy Elite (AAE)

ISC2019 conference awards in the General Non-fiction category and The Artists Music Guild's 2018 Author of the Year Award. The book was recognized as a Top Ten finalist with AAE where he presented his book on stage in front of his peers and attendees at the conference. His book was recognized as one of the top five authors covering all categories of music and the arts during the Artists Music Guild's 2018 Heritage Awards.

2018 Author Academy Elite
General Nonfiction

2018 Artists Music Guild
Author of the Year

Appendix A
Par for the Course

Life on the Golf Course - I retired from Corporate America in 2014 and after two years of dual residence management moved permanently to Elizabethtown, Kentucky. Since then, I have spent a lot of time on and around the Heartland Golf Course.

I had a lot of time on my hands as Kathy cherished her alone time reading novel after novel, therefore I was constantly being encouraged to go out and play golf. Once I started playing more often, I got to know the owners of the course and the limited staff who run the year-round operations; weather permitting. I began to volunteer around the course as an opportunity for me to meet more of the local crowd and to have something to do for eight hours a day. I was spending up to thirty hours a week working as a volunteer on the course. I took on more tasks and spent time: collecting range balls, serving as a course ranger, assisting with golf tournaments, fixing broken tools and equipment, retrieving broken down golf carts, as well as cleaning and filling the gas tanks before lining up the carts at night.

An added benefit to my constant presence at the golf course was that I was able to meet several of the groups of golfers who had been coming to the course for the past twenty plus years to play their own tournaments for three or four days during long weekends. After play, they intensely enjoyed their evenings in the pub located at the golf course. I had served as the daily starter when these groups arrived and often played with them during their afternoon round. On many occasions I traded gently used golf balls I had found for whatever beverages they carried on their carts. We classified that exchange as non-taxable bartering.

The Cincinnati Gang, as I called them, made their presence quickly. They were a happy and occasionally rowdy group. I spent more time with then than most groups through the summer. At the end of their golf adventure during the second week of June in 2018 they asked if I would be interested in preparing a Carolina Pork BBQ dinner for them in 2019. I subsequently planned and executed the Friday evening meal. Perhaps I had boasted of my culinary skills such that they were ready to challenge my "big talk." For $10 a man and a bottle of 18-year-old Glenlivet single-malt scotch, I prepared a full dinner for these thirty-two hungry golfers.

The 19ᵗʰ Hole Dinner menu:

1. 30 pounds of slow roasted Boston butt (pork shoulder)

    a. done three (3) ways
    b. one (1) pound of pork per person

2. 10 pounds of KFC recipe-style coleslaw
3. 10 pounds of egg potato salad
4. Chips
5. Rolls & butter
6. Homemade HOT! and mild BBQ sauce

The attendees provided their own assortment of refreshments, all with alcohol as their base.

From thirty pounds of pork shoulder to a pulled pork feast for 32

The Cincinnati Gang Golf Package – June 2019

Appendix B
Selected Recipes

I have included recipes from my favorite genres of cooking throughout the book and additional ones in the separate appendices. I purposefully did not include all of my creations, discoveries, experiments and adaptations because that would be well over two-hundred. I wanted to stay away from this becoming just another cookbook full of recipes and beautiful pictures of food. I decided at the beginning the format of this book would become:

1. More a documentation of my journey as a self-taught cook and some of the stories related to serving menus specifically prepared for the palette of other guests with the intent to share conversation. The desire to the share experiences and relationship that I have built through the process was the true goal.
2. A sharing of the recipes and pictures of my creations.

Obligatory Easter Dinner Pictures

MENU

Deviled Eggs
Broccoli Casserole
Green Beans / Bacon
Ham Gravy
Glazed Football Ham
Chilled Wine
Sweet Tea
Strawberries

Our daughter Erika insisted that I prepared the same dishes over and over again for each of the holidays when we get together. She and her mother don't like change or surprises. Tradition as they say. She knew what she liked and did not want unexpected offerings. Thanksgiving was always turkey, Easter was ham and Christmas combined the two, so we had ham and turkey. I was allowed to bake sweet potatoes for my own consumption. The sides dishes for every holiday meal were always the same: deviled eggs, broccoli casserole, green beans with bacon, homemade mashed potatoes and gravy, plus two kinds of cranberry sauce; jellied and whole berry.

One additional requirement was that I was had to cook more than we could eat in one sitting. Planning for leftovers were a necessary element in the process. No one goes home empty-handed from my house. We are not a big bread or dessert family, so they only appeared if we were hosting other guests at our holiday meal. However, there was always a gluten-free lemon meringue and/or gluten-free pumpkin pie for Kathy who suffers from Celiac disease (gluten intolerant).

Baked Chicken Transformed two ways

"Waste not, want not" they say. I'm not sure I know who said it first, but this proverb had to be created by someone's grandmother. Herbert Hoover ran on a platform declaring, "A chicken in every pot" almost 100 years ago in 1928. I never liked to waste food and I also enjoyed having different options when I prepared meals, especially when there are expected left-overs. Chicken was always an excellent choice for repurposing into a fantastic second meal option. Having the choice of dark verses light meat also provided different textures and tastes.

In this example I had baked a chicken in the oven at three-hundred-and-seventy-five degrees for one hour and forty-five minutes; after rubbing salt, pepper, paprika and Italian seasoning on the outside and had stuffed half an onion plus two stalks of cut celery in the body cavity.

Once the chicken was cooked, I allowed it to cool on the stove just barely long enough to be able to handle the bird with my bare hands. I separated the white meat from the dark meant and stored the breasts in the refrigerator for twenty-four hours. I preferred the wait time to ensure the meat didn't become soggy by adding the wet ingredients necessary to make chicken salad with warm meat.

Chicken salad recipe (one roasted chicken):
Cut baked chicken white meat into small cubes and put in a large mixing bowl
Add tablespoon of salt, a tablespoon of ground black pepper
Add teaspoon of paprika and then mix everything loosely
Wash and finely chop three to four celery stalks and place on top of chicken
Chop ¼ to ½ of a medium sweet onion (optional) and put on top of chicken
Blend celery and onion into chicken mixture
Add two teaspoons of lemon juice

Add ½ to 1cup of sweet pickle relish (drain the pickle juice first)

Add 2 cups of mayonnaise or salad dressing to the mixture (I prefer mayonnaise)

Gently fold and blend ingredients until completely mixed and chicken has been shredded

Taste and add additional relish, mayonnaise or salt/pepper as required for taste

Note: Some people prefer chunky chicken salad and others prefer the shredded option that looks much like tuna fish. If your preference is the chunky style then you should cut your chicken into larger cubes to start with, mix all your ingredients together except your chicken then gently fold the chicken cubes into the mixture. The final product will taste the same, it will just look different.

Chicken Salad and Spicy Pulled Chicken BBQ combo
The Two for One Option

Bacon wrapped center cut Pork Loin

This one is fairly easy to create. Purchase two or three center cut pork loins when they are on sale and put two in the freezer for later. Prepare one roast for a delicious meal served with fresh green beans, mashed potatoes and pork gravy made from scratch.

I like to use thick cut bacon for my wraps to ensure the juices from the roast remain intact. The thin cut bacon can be easier to work with so the option is one of preference and produces little difference in the final product as long as your lattice completely covers the roast.

Preparation and Cooking:

1. Create your favorite dry rub, coat the roast
2. Create lattice wrap of bacon and cover roast with the bacon securing with cooking twine
3. Wrap prepared roast in plastic wrap and let it marinade in the refrigerator twenty-four to forty-eight hours.
4. Remove from fridge and let stand on the stove for an hour to approach room temperature
5. Preheat oven to three-hundred-and-seventy-five degrees
6. Place on metal rack a deep sided pan and add two cups of water or chicken stock
7. Uncover roast, set it on the rack in the pan and place on middle rack in the oven
8. Cook for an hour and a half to two hours pulling the roast from the oven when it reaches 135 to 140 degrees
9. Cover with aluminum foil for fifteen to thirty minutes
10. Slice roast thinly, pour gravy over roast and mashed potatoes and enjoy

Lattice wrap center cut boneless pork loin with think cut bacon

Loin and bacon to keep bacon in place. Brown all sides 3-4 minutes in hot bacon dripping (grease)

Cook in center of heated oven at 375 degrees until pork in 135 degrees (appx. 1.5 hours)

Remove from oven, let rest for twenty minutes and slice to desired thickness

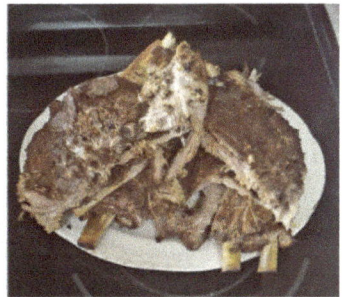

Applewood Oven Smoked Pork Ribs

Appendix C
Guest Cooks Contributions

Included in this section of the book is a small sampling of people and their personal creations for your review and consideration as an addition to your own cooking experiences. I want to thank my friends and contributors. Each was deeply engrossed in their developing careers yet have maintained the desire for cooking experiences and sharing their own stories with others.

BBQ'ers Gone Wild – Matthew Calderone and his Backyard Expressions

Matt's passion for cooking and conversations around the dinner able included many other self-described chefs and home cooks from a variety of backgrounds. This chapter is in his own words.

SMOKIN ANIMALS Smoked Meats – by Chef Matthew Calderone

Smoked Meats for BBQ Pork Recipe

Ingredients:
1 Pork Shoulder, Picnic, Butt (or 40), thawed if previously frozen, preference to larger cuts with the bone in and skin on, ~10lbs per piece
Yellow Mustard
Spices for rubbing (recipe based on rib rub from Central Barbecue in Memphis: https://cbqmemphis.com/products/seasoning, maintain ratio for larger quantities)

- Cumin – 1TBSP
- Paprika – 1TBSP
- Chili Powder – 1TBSP
- Kosher Salt – 2TBSP
- Granulated Onion – 1TBSP

- Granulated Garlic – 1TBSP
- Brown Sugar – 1TBSP
- Black Pepper – 1TSP
- White Pepper – 1TSP
- Cayenne Pepper – 1TSP

Apple Cider Vinegar and food safe spray bottle
King's Hawaiian Buns

Prep smoker with lots of wood,
bring meats to room temperature before beginning

Recipe:

1. Make preparations for smoking your pork piece(s) for 16-24 hours at 225 degrees
   a. Emphasis on hardwood smoking (logs if your rig can take them, wood chunks for a smaller offset barrel smoker, wood chips for an electric smoker)
   b. Using smoke boxes (or even foil pouches) for wood chips, just about any grill can be turned into a smoker

for the purposes of cooking a single pork piece, be creative, just don't use your oven

2. Mix your rub blend, feeling free to add additional ingredients to your liking (it's hard to get this part wrong)

3. On a large, flat surface place the pork piece on a large baking sheet

4. Pour a generous amount of yellow mustard on the pork piece and spread the mustard in a thin coat covering all surfaces

5. Sprinkle the rub over the surfaces of the pork piece, skin side down, no need to sprinkle rub on the skin side

Rubbed, On the Fire and completely smoked

6. Place the pork piece in your smoker and light the smoker

   a. The longer the meat receives smoke at a lower internal temperature, the more smoke it takes on, i.e. a colder (but not frozen) piece of pork at start will take on more smoke, same goes for the time it takes the smoker to achieve its temperature

7. Some smokers are very hard to control temperatures precisely on however pork is a very forgiving meat, temps between 175 and 325 throughout shouldn't alter the finished product much but try to maintain an average temperature of 225

   a. Wireless meat/chamber thermometers are your best friend in this cooking process

   b. If you are looking, it ain't cooking …

8. At steady intervals (every hour or two), spray the top of the pork piece with the apple cider vinegar, taking care to not let too much built up heat escape from the smoker if fuel and time efficiency is of concern

9. If your patience is waning and you aren't yet ready for the big leagues, once the meat reaches 140+ you can finish it in a roasting tray in your oven, wrapping in foil or peach butcher paper optional

10. As the pork piece approaches 209, pre-heat an oven to 170

11. The smoking is done when the pork's internal temperature reaches 209

12. Remove from the smoker and wrap in foil or peach butcher paper

13. Place the wrapped pork piece on a baking sheet in the pre-heated oven and turn the oven off, being certain to close the oven door afterwards

14. Let the pork rest for 4 hours allowing the juices to redistribute

15. Remove from oven and unwrap

16. Give the bone a gentle tug and it should glide right out, be careful to also remove any joints or cartilage that were formerly connected to the bone(s)

17. Place the pork in a sizeable mixing bowl and pull to your liking
    a. 2 large serving forks, meat claws or with your own hands using silicon gloves
    b. A KitchenAid® mixer on a low setting with the paddle attachment provides a consistent preparation every-time

18. Pour apple cider vinegar over the pulled pork to your liking

19. Serve on a plate, eaten with a fork or by making pulled pork sliders on a King's Hawaiian Bun, seasoning with additional Apple Cider Vinegar to your liking

a. I prefer heavily spiced vinegar-based sauces on my pulled pork but have yet to discover a national brand with a product worth recommending. A brand called "Scotts" from Goldsboro, NC can be found in supermarkets throughout the Carolinas and the Mid-Atlantic but otherwise I recommend buying a sauce you like at a local BBQ restaurant.

Rested, deboned and picked – ready for sauces

Matthew Calderone Bio: Matthew is a graduate of North Carolina State University with a degree in Electrical Engineering and has a Master's of Business Administration from the R.H. Smith School of Business, University of Maryland College Park. Matthew is a manager of engineering involved in Department of Defense (DOD) contracting and is working to grow his side hustle, meat smoking. When he isn't working or preparing delicacies of an animal nature, he loves traveling, golfing and following his Boston Red Sox, New England Patriots and NC State Wolfpack.

He never took to cooking growing up however was exposed to grilling and barbecue while attending college in Raleigh, North Carolina (Go Wolfpack!). In Raleigh, the term barbecue only means one thing and that is pulled pork with vinegar sauce (of course!). He never attempted his own pulled pork because it was so easy to find a side of the road shack or attend a pig pickin' on/near campus. Upon graduating and relocating to the mid-Atlantic, he developed a hankering for pulled pork and set out to create his own version of "down home North Carolina BBQ". Early attempts taking a large pork piece (shoulder/picnic/butt) and after fashioning a pouch out of several layers of tin foil, he filled the pouch with Scott's Barbecue Sauce (vinegar based) before sealing it all in. The pork was cooked over charcoal on a modest Weber Kettle® grill for about 4 hours, at temperatures of ~375 degrees.

After about 4 years of perfecting that technique/style, Matthew obtained his first smoker, a Chargriller® offset and that began his journey called "low and slow". The process was so very different and instead of being able to cook and serve in the same day, preparing pulled pork became a multi-day affair. The foil pouches were replaced by periodic spritzes of vinegar from a spray bottle and the pork itself took on the flavor of the charcoal and wood chunks in the smoker. To maximize the time investment, he quickly learned to smoke 50-60 pounds of pork at once, maxing out the capacity of the smoker. While employing the low and slow method of cooking the meat 16 to 20 hours, he still thoroughly doused the finished product in Scott's sauce producing pulled pork that was still very decidedly Eastern North Carolina Pulled Pork Barbecue. This recipe/preparation even beat the great Eric Pearson in a "pulled-pork-off" that he never thought he could lose to a Yankee!

On a visit to South Carolina to visit his parents at their new retirement home, He was exposed to South Carolina style "Barbecue" for the first time and boy; it could not have been more different! The pork itself was smoked without sauce/vinegar, and was served buffet style with a typical preparation being over a bed of Carolina Gold rice with a mustard-based sauce slathered on top of all. What really stood out to him was the smoke in the pork itself.

After about 8 years of doing his own thing on the Chargriller®, it rusted out and he was smoker-less for a time. A few years into really maximizing the Chargriller® to the fullest he had started to harbor ideas about procuring a towable "big boy" smoker and that dream was about to become a reality! He discovered an outfit outside Memphis, TN, Piggyback Smokers (www.piggyback-smokers.com), and had one custom made to his specifications out of a 250-gallon propane tank. Upon receipt and after an epic road trip to pick it up and discovering Memphis ribs, his barbecue journey was about to hit version 3.0. Smoking with whole hardwood logs, and he was finally able to hit the smoke content he had so fondly recalled from his South Carolina Barbecue experience. He tweaked his go-to rub to assimilate more of a Memphis dry-rub mixture. The smoke content coupled with the sweet/spicy rub and the semi-spicy vinegar sauce really is in a class of its own and something he continues to serve to friends, family and looks forward to satisfying customers for a long time to come! Matthew Calderone can be found on Facebook @ SMOKINANIMALS

The Ten-Minute Breakfast –
The Goen Indian Omelet – Nirdhar Khazanie

Nirdhar Khazanie (most often called Ninu) is of Indian descent, his family from Goa, India and he was one of my fantastic engineering hires from the period I led the New Graduate Development Program for Northrop Grumman during the years 2000 through 2010. I hired and led over two-thousand young engineers during that ten-year period. Just like Matt Calderone, Ninu was one of over two hundred other engineers I had discovered and recruited from the North Carolina State University campus. He had majored in electrical engineering and his family lived in Greenville, North Carolina.

Ninu became a great engineering entrepreneur, earned his master's degree in Computer Science from Johns Hopkins University, and after six years of "holding him back" while teaching him a thing or two along the way, I agreed to write a recommendation for him in his quest to join Google. I was excited to be a small part in his development to move to the desire to work at Google, where he probably belonged all along.

I was fortunate to be invited to his wedding in Indianapolis, Indiana and had the pleasure of experiencing three days and nights of nonstop events with the foods of India everywhere I turned. It was a tremendous experience, one I'll never forget, and an honor to be immersed into a culture I had not experienced prior to the event. I have to admit I was surprised to see Ninu ride a horse completely around the hotel to make his grand entrance as the opening act of the ceremony.

Nirdhar Khazanie
riding to his wedding

His dedication and love for food, creating recipes and publishing pictures of his creations became one of my motivations to continue my own pursuit and write this book. We spoke for many hours about food, the creation of special dishes and how to balance the combinations of spices to enhance rather than overpower a meal. Combining his love for food and his software engineering background, Ninu developed an application for phones that would allow anyone to type in the ingredients in one's refrigerator and out would come a choice of recipes to make for lunch or dinner. I asked to share two of his personal recipes; the first is not your simple Sunday Omelette.

Ninu would often stop by my office and ask, "What are you doing for lunch"? knowing quite well I seldom went out to eat. I would nod my head and his response was always, "Come with me, I've found a new place you need to try, you are going to love it." Every time it was somewhere out of a Middle Eastern region and as he walked in the door, the owner would yell out his name and give him a bear hug. I always let him order the food and often we would sample ten to twenty different items from a lunch buffet. The food was always great and had it not been for Ninu's passion, I expect would still be eating peanut butter and jelly sandwiches.

From Nirdhar, "Since I can remember, my parents have made variations of this omelet and it's one of my favorite breakfast foods on a lazy Saturday morning. The best part is it really does take only 10 minutes. My mom doesn't usually add the coconut but I find it adds a different flavor most people aren't expecting."

The 10-minute Goan Indian Omelette

Details of the 10-miute Goan Indian Omelette Nirdhar Khazanie – ninu at https:// foodfame.com
Prep time: 5–7 minutes
Cook Time: 3 minutes
Serves: 2 people

Tips while cooking this dish:
- Try to use Portobello mushrooms as the coarseness adds a hearty texture
- Use fresh ground masala rather than a pre-packaged one if possible (spice grinders destroy the flavor with the heat emitted from it. Yes, it's time consuming but the aroma and flavor isn't present)

Ingredients
Spices
1/4 tsp cumin seeds
1 in of a cinnamon stick
4 black peppercorn seeds
2 cardamom pods (peeled)
1/2 tsp salt
1/2 tsp paprika powder
1/2 tsp turmeric
1/8 tsp fennel seeds
1/8 tsp coriander seeds

Mix all of these spices inside a mortar & pestle until the texture resembles one of coarse sand. About 30 seconds' total time.

Raw Ingredients
Per person use {3 eggs—1 full egg, 2 egg whites}
1 medium yellow onion, minced
1 green chili minced (use less if you can't tolerate the heat)
1 Roma tomato, chopped
1 small handful of coriander leaves, chopped (keep them flaky with life, try not to mince them)
1 Portobello mushroom, chopped
2 tsp shredded coconut

Directions

1. Beat the eggs in a mixing bowl with a fork until fluffy.
2. Mix in the raw ingredients.
3. Pour in the spices from the mortar & pestle and lightly fold the eggs into the masala. Lightly mix everything together.
4. Keep a nonstick pan on medium heat, use olive oil and lightly cook the first side until it's lightly browned.
5. Flip over and sprinkle a bit of salt to your taste.

There you have it; My grandmother's The Ten Minute Goan Omelette- Nirdhar Khazanie

Tandoori Salmon – Nirdhar Khazanie

Because he has such a passion for food Ninu has developed a great repertoire of cooking styles and dishes and I wanted to share one of my favorites Ninu created with salmon and the main dish. Typically, we don't eat enough fish and perhaps by trying the recipe the pattern will change. Notice how little prep time and cooking time is involved with this dish. So, pick up the special spices next time you are at the grocery store and stop by the fish market on your way home from work or play; give this one a try, you'll love it.

Tandoori Salmon with Garlic & Honey in Olive Oil

Recipe:
Prep time: 5 min
Cook Time: 3 min
Serves: 2 people (can be scaled up one-for-one for dinner guests)
Tips while cooking this dish:
- pinch the fish and draw 2–3 slits to keep the flesh from folding upwards
- do not flip more than 2 xs, allow to rest in the olive oil and be patient

Ingredients
Spices
1 tsp kosher salt
1/2 tsp fresh cracked black pepper
1 clove of garlic minced
1/4 tsp Raja brand tandoori masala (my mom trusts this brand)
2 tsp honey
Raw Ingredients
2 hearty salmon fillets

Directions:

1. Season the fish with kosher salt and set aside for 5 min.
2. Use a nonstick pan and pour in olive oil allowing it come to a medium-high temperature, add the minced garlic.
3. Carefully place the fish (skin side down) on the pan and allow it to cook for about 1 min until the color starts changing 1/2 way from the bottom to the top of the fish.
4. Quickly sprinkle tandoori masala, pepper, salt, and flip over.
5. Allow the fish to cook for around 30–45 sec more on high heat then carefully remove the fish from the pan and let it cool for 2 min before service.

There you have it, Tandoori Salmon with Garlic & Honey in Olive Oil. Serve it with a heart rice dish and a steamed vegetable such as broccoli, green beans or spinach with a side salad and you have a hearty, tasty, lean complete meal.

Gluten Free Taco Salad by Ronald David Re – In his own words

Ronald David Re is an author like me who has journeyed into the art of writing and publishing his works through the Author Academy Elite (AAE) program. He posted a creation on Facebook that he had assembled from ingredients found in his refrigerator and asked the public to recommend an appropriate name. I suggested Gluten Free Taco Salad and we suddenly became joined in our quests for the love of cooking. Here is his story behind his creation.

"My passion for food and cooking came through the varied years of experience that makes up my journey. I've had relatives in health care that have evidence that our food is making us sick. I have also enjoyed vegetables cooked in a variety of ways that make any meal delicious. I usually can make something healthy and simply with a little planning and thought. I have a farmer in the family and learned how genetically modified organisms (GMO) food is farmed and how the typical farmer that creates food for quantity and not quality.

If it is our diet that is making us sick then we need to eat healthier food. It can be like medicine to our bodies. Also, my spiritual belief is that God designed food that is good for us and our body craves real unaltered fresh food. Part of the issue is having a regular supply of fresh vegetables in your fridge and being prepared.

Here is an example of a dish I created with what we had on hand and what was in the garden. A few tips for healthy ingredients. Buy a large tub of coconut oil online, you can use if for everything including cooking! Buy garlic already minced in the jar. It is too good for your body to not have on hand. Plant a garden; soon you will sport free groceries with a little sweat equity. Buy green stuff- Must have things like mixed greens; kale, spinach etc. (eat daily). Know what you can buy in bulk and they will last, like onions.

Just because I had these ingredients on-hand I made the following breakfast:

Gluten Free Taco Salad –

The cool:

Slice tomatoes and put in a circle format around your plate.

Sprinkle cottage cheese on top of tomatoes, and then add olive oil around the ring.

Top with salt and pepper to taste.

The hot:

Sautee with Coconut oil: onions, spinach, garlic, peppers, and mushrooms.

Scramble in 4 large eggs

Sprinkle shredded cheddar cheese on top.

Put the hot in the middle of the circle and eat up, (serves 2) Enjoy!"

Gluten-free Taco Salad   *Author of CHOSEN to be Blessed*

Poor Folk Spaghetti/chili meal – by Marsha Marcum

This story is quite special to me. It did not start as a conversation over a meal, yet it became one many years later. It all began over ten years ago during the annual conference for the Southern Association of Colleges and Employers (SoACE). I presented SoACE in different section of the book, so I'll only mention the connection with Marsha Marcum. Our annual conference was held at the Gaylord Opryland Resort and Conference Center in Nashville, Tennessee.

The highlight of each week's agenda was always the entertainment the last night of the conference. That year the entertainment committee kept our guest performer a secret and with trumpets blaring, Dolly Parton entered Center Stage where she delivered a fantastic show. Only, it was Marsha Marcum who did the honors that evening, Dolly was unable to attend. I was only able to speak with her for a few minutes after the performance because the crowd to meet and greet her was over five-hundred strong. We all know how Groupies can be.

Fast forward more than ten years later, I was serving on the Board of Directors of The Artists Music Guild, thought of Marsha's performance and nominated her for Artist of the Year, Singer of the Year and Song of the Year. She was unable to attend the awards program though I kept in contact. We stayed in touch through Facebook, like everybody else, and she has offered me advice on buying properties here in Kentucky. I also have her CDs that I play all the time on long trips in the car.

I saw her post on the Po Folk Main Dish as I was completing my final edit of the book and just knew I had to include Marsha in the section on guest Chefs.

615-977-9373
marshamarcum32@yahoo.com

Marsha is an outstanding Realtor from Murfreesboro, Tennessee, offers her services to entire Nashville area and it seems she is the #1 producer month after month, year after year. She is one of the few people I know who can not only sing for her supper, but cook it as well.

Po Folk Spaghetti/Chili

Ingredients lined up and ready to go

In her own words since it's her recipe. "Some of my friends and family have called me over the phone to get this recipe from me. I call it my Poor folk spaghetti/chili meal.
Assembly Required:

1. Hamburger or turkey in skillet
2. Chop onion, bell peppers in with meat.
3. once the meat is almost cooked, put in mushrooms, salt, pepper, seasoning salt, and packets of seasoning, add fresh tomatoes 🍅 or substitute canned tomatoes and canned chili beans, but fresh is better. I use left-over cooked brown beans.
4. Poor in spaghetti sauce and let it cook for about 20 minutes on low.

5. in a separate pan, cook your angel hair spaghetti and add a little butter so that it doesn't boil over and/or stick together.

6. Once cooked, drain the water off and add about 3 TBS of olive oil.

7. In a separate baking pan, pour spaghetti into dish, add sauce, more spaghetti and add sauce. Layer it.

8. Add shredded cheese then top it off with sliced pepperoni.

9. Bake in the oven for another 20-30 minutes on 350.

The portions of ingredients depend on how many people you are serving. It will stick to your ribs for hours or years." – Marsha Marcum

Appendix G for Gluten free cooking experience

Gluten-free: It's not for everyone

After we discovered in her late 30's that my wife's Kathy had suffered from undiagnosed Chron's disease since high school, we changed many of our eating habits. She worked closely with our Gastroenterologist, Dr. Richard Chassen, to create a better life through: nutrition, diet, exercise and taking all things in moderation. Her immune system had been damaged and was susceptible to bouts of inflammation and other symptoms that led her to often having to skip meals rather than deal with the after-effects. On top of that, one day we discovered Kathy was gluten intolerant and tested positive for Celiac Disease. Over time, the immune reaction to eating gluten creates inflammation that damages the small intestine's lining, leading to medical complications. It also prevents absorption of some nutrients (malabsorption).

The classic symptom is diarrhea. Other symptoms include bloating, gas, fatigue, low blood count (anemia), and osteoporosis. Many people have no symptoms. The mainstay of treatment is a strict gluten-free diet that can help manage symptoms and promote intestinal healing. Over 200,000 people in the United States are found to be gluten intolerant each year.

We began a regime that completely eliminated breads and wheat from our diets, I gave away the four bread machines I held in my inventory and began the search for gluten free flours, recipes and options to supplement the loss of bread in my diet. One can only eat so much rice after having grown up eating Wonder Bread® my entire life.

Celiac disease had been identified as long ago as the 1ˢᵗ Century A.D. Yes, a very long time ago. However, it did not gain prominence until the early 19th Century until there was critical research conducted in the 1980's through the 1990's. The alternatives to gluten rich breads, pastries, pies and the like were few, far between and expensive. Suddenly because of the publicity of celiac disease and the rush to jump on the next "band wagon" the availability of ingredients in the stores and restaurant foods brought the cost down significantly. Though still expensive, at least many choices became available for those who had suffered many years from the rarely publicized disease.

I tried many of the options recommended, flours and ingredients in the small and expensive section of the grocery store and also "searched the world over for my true love". It was difficult, the recipes were touted as perfect solutions, yet I found then next to impossible to replicate. Instead of flour and yeast, I was to use Xanthan Gum, which caused my creations to be doughy and thick, did not rise and created gummy messes. It seems that folding and blending xanthan gum into traditional recipes was more of an art than a science. I even tried using grated and fried cauliflower as the base. It worked but was far too time consuming.

Though I continued to push the envelope on my baking skills and preparing gluten free dishes, I have decided to limit my efforts and concentrated on my more successful genres: pork BBQ, smoking meats, stews, slow-cooker creations and casseroles.

Here are a few of my personal, though moderate successes at creation gluten free meals with alternative replacements for the gluten. If you want to try the easiest one first, give gluten free pancakes your first effort. It's made with bananas instead of flour.

2 Ingredient Gluten Free Pancakes
1 ripe banana
2 large eggs

Cooking Instructions
Mash banana with a fork; mush
Whip the eggs with a fork

Combine banana & eggs
Spoon 2 tbls. On buttered griddle
Flip after ½1 to 2 min – slow flip
Cook 1 additional minute
Top with butter & syrup
Stack pancakes and eat warm

Gluten free pancakes

Gluten free biscuits

Gluten free spinach &
Country ham quiche

Gluten free chicken pot pie

Gluten free meatloaf

As the gluten free options for flour substitutes have improved, I began using and experimenting with different "box mixes" and modifying the quantity of adds such as milk, eggs, butter to increase the fluffiness while attempting to get biscuits, cakes and rolls to rise like normal ones.

I found it difficult because the xanthan gum tends to create a heavy binder and clog up, the dough becomes spongy, and it does not cook evenly. The mixture sets such that instead of rising it falls flat and becomes chewy. So, be careful, blend your ingredients slowly. Do not use a stand mixer on anything but low and once it appears blended, stop and start the next step.

Flat griddle

Gluten free pancakes (modified recipe)

Since I am from Maryland (1966 – 2016) and we are known for the world's best steamed blue crab I created this breakfast treat. The presentation gives one the appearance of Maryland crabs as the breakfast of gluten free pancakes and bacon, bacon, bacon. Of course, it must be smothered with butter on every layer and drenched in pure maple syrup.

The modification I chose in preparing and cooking the mix was managed by adding an extra egg and an extra tablespoon of milk and an extra tablespoon of oil to the recipe. This resulted in fluffier pancakes. I poured approximately 1/4 cup of the mix on a lightly oiled 350-degree griddle, and gently spread the mixture out to eliminate high spots. I discovered that thinner the better with this one. Then I proceeded to cook the pancakes on one side until the edges became brown, flipped and cooked for another minute or two. I was able to cook three pancakes at a time and recommend you do not crowd the griddle.

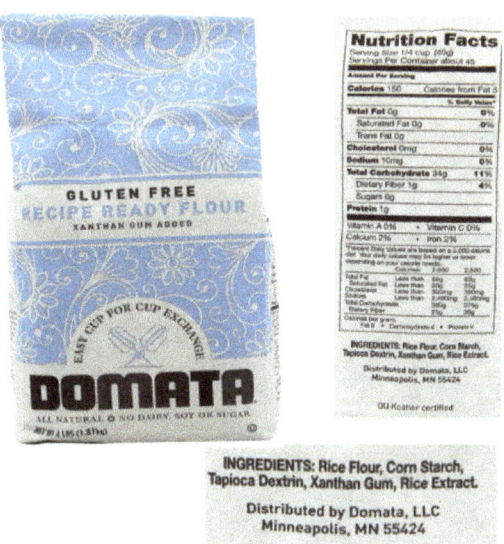

INGREDIENTS: Rice Flour, Corn Starch, Tapioca Dextrin, Xanthan Gum, Rice Extract.

Distributed by Domata, LLC
Minneapolis, MN 55424

After trying many gluten-free products, I chose Domata as my go to source for gluten free flower. It used to be available on the shelf at Kroeger, but since I had early luck, I have had to order it online from the source most recently.

I found creating my own self-rising flour required several ingredients, significant time and I could not develop any consistency. I know people use rice flower and almond flower. They are much more expensive and I could not produce the desired results.

The stages of creating Mouth-watering
Gluten Free Turkey Pot Pie

Creamy broth with gluten free flour, peas, carrots, celery, onions, blended with 1 & ½ pounds of cubed cooked turkey

*Lattice top gluten free pastry on top
And gluten free pastry sheet on bottom*

Baked at 425 degrees for 45 minutes
Carefully broiled for 4 to 6 minutes until golden brown

Gluten Free Mac & Cheese – Schar Fusilli noodles

Appendix H

Roasting a Homo sapiens - in the rhetorical sense

As I sat adding the icing to the final stories for this book and began to assemble the many recipes along with associated pictures that had I developed over the years, I received a text message from my friend, Michael Alvarez, The Mayor of Indian Train, North Carolina. I had recently sent him a check for a contribution to his campaign as he was running for a third term as "Mayor of the People for the People and of course by the People". Recently I sent his $2,000 to help pay for his prostatic are to replace the one he lost to cancer. He will be the first to admit he doesn't like raising money though he is quite good at it when he represents The Artists Music Guild (AMG) and all the work they do in the community to foster artistic education in Title I schools and offer many children's programs.

Michael wasn't asking for a larger donation, instead he requested I leave the comforts of Elizabethtown, Kentucky, fly to the Charlotte, North Carolina and 'roast' him for his fiftieth birthday party. Since I had become a well-known chef (in my own mind at least), would I come and celebrate with him and all of his constituents, family and friends? He was running for Mayor of Indian Trail and preparing the push to gather votes for his re-election intended to place his name and face in the win column at the same time.

I found this request to be one of great honor, readily accepted and quickly began to prepare the Alvarez Seven Course Menu to roast him until he was done medium-well; the audience was expected to be rolling in the aisles. Some of the attendees would be targeted as well; because that's the way a roast goes these days. The tribute was well received, full of comic relief and laughter and once I cut five pages out of the twenty-six-page, 4,987-word tribute, it lasted only twenty-eight minutes. If it had been any longer, I would have had to schedule a bathroom break much like the original showing of *Ben Hur* at the movie theaters in 1959 that ran 212 minutes; yes 3 hours and 32 minutes.

Michael, I love you man. Cherish the words that played well, and quickly forget the ones that were met with boo, ah, or Oh My! I did everything I could to raise your spirits and increase your re-election war chest and did no imagine the joke of passing a paper bag around with your picture on it would actually net $37.17 in donations to your campaign for Mayor.

Appendix R for Roadkill

You can never make it taste like chicken

! WARNING!
There are State and Federal laws regarding the acquisition and consumption of wild animals... A simple picking up of a squirrel, taking it home and preparing a snack might get you in trouble. Please check your state regulations if you feel determined to take the plunge into wild game entrees.
!WARNING!

Roadkill – Look twice before crossing the road

Raccoons on our deck in Maryland

Eat them before they eat you

Twenty States allow the harvesting of roadkill- as of 10/10/2019

Alabama	only non-protected animals and game animals during open season may be harvested)
Alaska	individuals are not allowed to harvest animals, but moose, caribou, and other species may be distributed through volunteer organizations
Arizona	big game animals may be collected with permit
Arkansas	no restrictions
Colorado	proper authorization required)
Georgia	native species may be harvested; notify state for road killed black bears
Idaho	must report the time of the salvage
Illinois	proper hunting or trapping license and/or habitat stamp required
Indiana	permit required
Maryland	permit required
Massachusetts	permit required; must submit roadkill for state inspection
Michigan	deer and bear may be salvaged with permit

New Hampshire	no restrictions
New York	license or tag may be required depending on species
New Jersey	only deer may be salvaged with permit
North Dakota	permit required
North Carolina	must be registered over the phone by DNR staff
Ohio	no restrictions
Oregon	no restrictions
Pennsylvania	must report the incident to state game commission within 24 hours
South Dakota	proper notification and authorization required
Tennessee	no restrictions
Utah	permit required to salvage non-protected species
Vermont	possession tag required for big game animals and furbearers
Washington	no restrictions
West Virginia	must be reported within 12 hours of collection
Wisconsin	must be registered over the phone by DNR staff
California*	at the printing of this book, in the process of approval

Credit WIDE OPEN eats – Maria Cristina Lake 4/2/2019

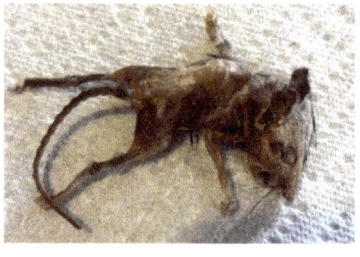

Petrified Mouse – All Roadkill has a shelf-life
For Display Only – "not for human consumption"

I had watched several shows on life in America and the "made for television" one-hour series on things people do for a living around the world. One included a couple of episodes on trapping unwanted house guests, called critters of a variety of species: raccoons, snakes, possum, wild boar, rats, mice, bats, bees, squirrels, gators and the like. Having been a life-science and biology teacher back in the early 1980's, I found these shows entertaining and when a show came on about eating wild animals and roadkill, I was drawn to investigate the possibilities at a deeper level. I have included my new found knowledge in the book. In conducting my research, I even found several opportunities to experience roadkill on a personal level.

After completing my research, I learned that there are more places and people than I thought possible where roadkill meals are prepared and consumed. Often roadkill served as a major dietary necessity in some families' lifestyle. They had perfected the art of acquiring the fresh-killed entrées, developed their own skinning and gutting processes, preparation techniques for consumption required via heavily marination and a salting procedure prior to the practiced culinary completion of fine dining in the far reaches of the country, swamp, desert and other "off the road" living locations. Yes, that sentence was a mouthful.

My wife Kathy's family grew up in the country of Kentucky where both of her grandparents lived on farms and the weekly family gathering after church on Sunday brought a gang of people together to share a pot luck meal that was laid out for all to enjoy. She never asked what was for dinner because it could just as well have been a squirrel, possum, weasel, muskrat, dove, pigeon, snake and a cow culled from the herd out in the field. Her grandmother Lewis promised they never served rats, bats or mice to guests; family included.

I understood that one could tell the difference between hunted meat and fresh roadkill. If it had been hunted you most likely would spend some time picking buckshot out of your dinner entrée prior to cooking.

Let's get back to the topic of this chapter and my personal roadkill experiences, the period of time I spent in El Segundo, California. When I had a free time, I would drive up the coast to Cambria and spend the weekend camping, overlooking the Pacific Coast at Camp Ocean Pines. It had been a favorite location for our semi-annual Experiential Leadership Development Program Summits. The Camp Executive Directors, Chris and Rosemary Cameron had been responsible for having created a long history of establishing and growing the camp.

Chris was a trained Naturalist, taught certification classes throughout the year and had become a Falconer where he took young hawks, raised and trained them for hunting and most he released back into the wild. Chris would take fresh roadkill (sans maggots), freeze them and feed them to the resident owl, the resident eagle, and use pieces in training his new falcons. I mentioned on one trip to the camp where Chris allowed me to feed the owl and eagle that had often seen fresh kill on the roadside during the three-hour drive up from Los Angeles. His eyes brightened up and said, "Eric, don't miss a chance to scoop up the roadkill, I'll clean it, freeze it and feed it to the birds, small bites at a time." He promised me that he did not use any of it for human consumption.

That day began my concerted three-year search and retrieval of fresh roadkill for Camp Ocean Pines. I always carried a backpack that contained a flashlight, clear trash bags, paper towels, wipes and a hunting knife in case the roadkill was larger than a jackrabbit. There were times when I would catch a glimpse of potential treasure as I flashed down the highway. I would quickly circle back the mile or so to investigate and retrieve the next meal for the birds.

I no longer work in California therefore my days of hunting roadkill are over however Chris and I stay in contact more than ten years later and when I pass roadkill on the highway, I definitely think to myself, "Chris would like that. Perhaps I should pick it up, quick freeze it and ship it to Cambria, California packed in dry ice." Kathy would not approve, so I now keep my noble thoughts to myself. Though in October of 2019 I saw: a hare, an opossum, an armadillo, a raccoon and a coyote on the side of the road during a five-hour drive through Arizona that would have served well as roadkill dinner.

Larry would have wanted it this way, he always said, "Don't waste a good meal"

Once I saw a turkey buzzard being picked clean by other turkey buzzards. Now that was a sight to see; cannibalism right there beside the open highway. It has to be inspiration for a future Gary Larson Cartoon. Just picture one turkey buzzard lying dead along the side of the highway with several other turkey vultures standing around. I created the above cartoon to represent the experience.

I had often live-trapped and relocated possums and groundhogs that had moved in under our shed or dug caverns around the pool deck at our home in Ellicott City, Maryland. Shortly after watching an episode on roadkill cooking, I decided I would use a kill trap for a groundhog who had taken residence under our storage shed while I was in the process of selling our Maryland house and moving permanently to Elizabethtown, Kentucky. It was time to join Kathy and aging dogs. The purpose of the experiment was to take this one chance to prepare and eat a wild animal that fit the roadkill requirements. I set the trap and two days later I found my prize, safe and secure in the grips of the trap. Just to be clear, there were no domestic animals injured during this event. The only problem was, that instead of catching a large and robust groundhog I had assumed was living under my shed, it was a small groundhog; one too small to invest the time and effort to properly prepare and cook. Instead, I cut it into manageable pieces, put in the deep-freezer and shipped it off the Cambria to feed the resident eagles and owls. Sometimes well-placed plans result in a better solution. Besides, I have since discovered that there are rules about collecting and disposal of roadkill. You can't just find it, collect it, cook it and eat it. In most States you must report a roadkill incident and have a permit to retrieve and eat said animal.

"Be flexible", one of my high school teachers used to spout, now I had realized what Mrs. Miller meant; but not sure how that ever applied to Geometry Class back in 1963. Hers was a class after lunch, therefore I often slept through class and still managed to earn a 96 average and an "A" for the year (94 was a B). Mrs. Miller seems to fit in the book because her class was right after lunch. Roadkill Chefs United, perhaps I should start the Facebook Group and see how it marinates and develops into a full-fledged seven-course meal type of conversations.

The Journey ends at the Road Kill Café

A fitting end to my negotiating through food and people happened by accident. Kathy and I, actually Kathy, planned a trip to Las Vegas for us to see her favorite group in concert; The Eagles (not the football team). We flew in early, drove to Kingman, Arizona for a night, spent one night on the South Rim of the Grand Canyon, one night back in Kingman on the way back to Vegas and finally one night at the MGM Grand for the concert.

After spending the night in Kingman and eating at the In-N-Out Burger joint, we drove on to the Canyon. As we approached Seligman, Arizona, Kathy asked if I would stop and get her a bottle of water, knowing I didn't like stopping on the road to anywhere, but it was her vacation so we pulled off the Interstate and onto the famous Rt. 66, took a left-hand turn and directly in front of us was the Road Kill Café. What a fitting surprise since I had already begun writing my final chapter for the book titled, *Cooking Road Kill – You can never make it taste like chicken.*

As if it was an act of God, or more likely and accidental occurrence, I had found the ending to this book and proceeded to introduce myself. I explained my purpose to the Manager, Patty, and requested permission to include the Road Kill Café story for your personal enjoyment as well. So here it is.

22830 W. Hwy 66, Seligman, AZ, October 4, 2019

Roadkill 66 Café – "Welcome to the Roadkill Café, and adventure in dining! They are famous for its char-broiled Burgers, Buffalo Burgers, and steaks. The Roadkill Café – OK Saloon is definitely well worth the stop along Route 66. Eating is more fun when you know it was a hit on the run! Our menu has a great selection to choose from, and we are sure to have something for everyone! There's a great opportunity to take pictures and shop around for Souvenirs in The Famous OK Saloon. It is filled with all kinds of antiques from the area's "old west" past.

Located just outside is the old Arizona Territorial Jail whose walls once corralled such notorious outlaws as Seligman Slim, Four Fingers Frank and the legendary Carl "Curry" Bane. Standing next to the jail is a replica of some old west store fronts that have been the background for many commercials and documentaries filmed in the area."

Credit the Roadkill 66 Café Menu.
22830 W. Hwy. 66, P.O. Box. 5, Seligman, AZ,

About The Roadkill Café

"Jim and Jean Pope married in 1947 and had four children. In 1964, the family moved from the east coast to California. On the way they spent a night here in Seligman at the Navajo Motel (now known as the Historic Route 66 Motel). The family settled in Westminster California where they owned and operated a family catering truck business.

In 1983, the family sold their business and bought several other businesses in Seligman, Arizona. One of those businesses was the Navajo Motel (now known as Historic the Route 66 General Store that the family had stayed in twenty years earlier. They also bought the Historic Route 66 General Store, Route 66 Automotive and Towing, and a small bar called the OK Saloon. A patio was added to the front of the building to hold parties and dances. In 1997, the patio was enclosed and the Roadkill Café was born. Some people still remember the early days when the menu was much smaller and patrons could wear chef hats and grill their own steaks. As you can see the restaurant and its menu have grown quite a bit since then.

Jim passed away in 2004 and Jean in 2016. Their children, DeeDee, Debbie and Bill continue running the business today with the help from some of Jim and Jean's grandchildren, great-grandchildren and many wonderful employees. Their dream continues."

Credit Roadkill 66 Café Menu.
22830 W. Hwy. 66, P.O. Box. 5, Seligman, AZ,

Roadkill 66 Breakfast Menu Items

Name	*Description*
Awesome Possum	A traditional breakfast
Roadside Revenge	Steak & Eggs
Creamed Quail on Toast	Egg and cheese on an English muffin
Splatter Platter	Chicken fried steak breakfast
Smear of Dear	Biscuits and Gravy
Guess the Mess	Roadkill's Famous Skillet
Rigor Mortise Tortoise	Hungry Man Breakfast
Dead Meat Treat	Denver Omelette
Armadillo on the Half Shell	Breakfast Burritos
One Eyed Dog Hit in the Frog	Texas Style French toast
Buzzard Bait	Chorizo Plate

Credit the Roadkill 66 Café Menu.
22830 W. Hwy. 66, P.O. Box. 5, Seligman, AZ,
(928) 422-3554 www.route66seligmanaz.com

End of the line Recipe – "The Roadkill Café"

I found it most fitting that the last two recipes in the book come from the Roadkill Café. As I was wrapping up the ending to this journey I received a call from Debbie Mejia, the owner. We had a nice half-hour phone conversation discussing the book. She provided me additional details about her family of four generations in the food industry and their own journey surrounded by food and people. Their culinary journey drove them from the East Coast of the United States to food trucks in Westminster, California and eventually to Seligman, Arizona where they continue the wonderful experiences with people and food at The Roadkill Café.

Here are Debbie's two favorite recipes from their menu. Stop and enjoy a great meal and historical conversation at the end of the famous Rt. 66. Don't forget to tell them, Eric sent you.

Rack of Raccoons (St. Louis Ribs)
By Debbie Mejia, Owner, in her own words

We use only the best USDA (Grade A) Pork Ribs.

In a large (12" x 21") rectangular pan, place racks of ribs side by side (meat side up).

Then we drown them with a 1/2 gallon of our secret Roadkill BBQ sauce.

Next, we fill the pan with water, slice up 3 Navel Oranges and place them a top.

Cover pan and bring to a boil, then reduce heat to low and cook for at least 2 hours until tender
(Meat will almost be falling off of the bones).

Then we drain juices off and place them bones on a hot char-broiler (or at home the BBQ).

Cook for about 3 to 4 minutes on each side.

Slather both sides with more of the secret Roadkill BBQ sauce and serve with plenty of Wet Naps!

Monkey Soup (Young Buzzards Favorite)
By Debbie Mejia, Owner, in her own words

2 Pounds of fresh "Roadkill" (your choice - we use
    ground meat)
6 stacks of Celery
2 large Carrots
15 ounce can Tomato Sauce
4 - 5 Fresh Diced Tomatoes
1 1/2-ounce Seasoning Salt
6 - 8 Cups Water

Brown your choice of ground "Roadkill". Then drain.

In a big pot, add meat, celery, carrots, tomato sauce, diced tomatoes, seasoning salt and water.

Bring to a very hot boil, and then reduce to a simmer.

Cook until carrots and celery are tender.

Garnish with your favorite Hot Sauce and enjoy.

The Roadkill Café Revisited – Friends and Family unite

A young friend of mine and extremely giving person from The Artists Music Guild, Nils Bundy, was finally able to save enough money to take his husband on a week vacation after attending the funeral for his own grandfather. He mentioned they were going to fly to Vegas for a few days and wanted to know what to go see in the area. I suggested The Hoover Dam, The Grand Canyon and The Roadkill Café that was situated half-way between the two.

On their way back from the Grand Canyon on Sunday, February 14th (Valentine's Day) they stopped in Seligman at the Roadkill Café for lunch. I instructed him to see if one of the owners was there and if so, let me speak to her on the phone. She was there and we spent fifteen minutes on the phone catching up with their efforts running the town (they owned just about all of it), the process in completing this book, and I explained about my friends Niles. She said, "Don't worry, I'll take care of them."

Nils and Allen at The Roadkill Café with one of the owners

Niles excitedly called me three times during lunch to tell me what they were eating. After lunch, Nils called again and explained the rest of what they had for lunch and how well they were taken care of. I told him that when he went up to pay for their lunch, call me and hand the phone to the owner, because I wanted to pay for their Valentine's Day lunch. He handed me the phone and when I explained to the owner what I wanted to do she said, "No charge, I already told you that we would take care of them." I had no idea that's what she meant.

If you are ever on the road from Kingman, AZ to the Grand Canyon, stop at The Roadkill Café, mention my name, there is no telling what kind of reception you might receive.

Epilogue

After all the stories have been told; "It's a wrap"!

What's Cookin' became a dream of mine during the three years I spent in El Segundo, California; between December 2011 and October 2014. I spent most of my time during that period working and as a guest of The Residence Inn. As I began the journey to enhance my skills as a self-taught chef with the aid of the Chopped series on The Food Channel, I decided that I would begin documenting my conversations over food, my experiences cooking recipes I pulled from the internet, modified recipes I found or knew of to blend my own style of cooking to properly season the realm of my cooking experiences. I decided in 2011 that I was going to attempt to document my version of the journey of cooking through words and pictures.

I retired from Northrop Grumman on September 30, 2014 and moved back to our home in Ellicott City, Maryland; intending to transition to our retirement home in Elizabethton, Kentucky as soon as possible. Over the following two years we transitioned to our retirement home in my wife's hometown. During the transition period I began and completed my second book titled, *The People You meet in First Class: When Chance Meetings Become Life Changing Conversations.* As I completed and published that book, I began to assemble the stories and search my picture library for which of my many creation meals I would include in *What's Cookin'.*

When I started collecting my recipes and stories for this book, I had planned to just telling stories about my cooking experience and the people I had met through my outgoing personality and self-proclaimed status as a home-gown chef. I had figured that we all had to eat, therefore there must be a common bond between each and every one of us. Language barriers were quickly broken by universal words like yum. In many cultures belching is seen as a sign of compliment. I was only going to refer to some of my creations that surrounded the personal interactions, while not including more than a few recipes and pictures.

The book was initially planned and structured to be 20,000 +/- words and perhaps I might provide a separate download of the recipes and pictures I gathered and modified over the years. As was my journey through life unplanned and of limited structure, I found that the development of this book also became far different than the plan. The reader instead has found the history of my cooking journey, stories that encouraged me to continue my quest as well as pictures and recipes of some of my more enterprising creations.

I thought my experience was complete when I retired in 2014, only to realize my passion for cooking surrounded by people and their experiences continued and I finally forced myself to end the journey of adding new stories and recipes on October 5, 2019 and forced myself to proceed with completion, editing and release of my treasured manuscript.

Then COVID19 happened, shutting all of us down and when schools opened for in-class instruction the beginning of January of 2021, I was called by the local Middle school and asked to complete a long-term substitute assignment in 7th grade English, Reading and Journalism classes. I accepted expecting that by the end of January they would have hired a Certified English Language Arts teacher. They became comfortable with me taking over and creating the curriculum for 127 students and I was roped into completing the school year with my last day being May 28, 2021. I lost the six months I had planned to complete my book but enjoyed a wonderful time engaging with, and teaching students about language and the arts. So, now its July of 2021, I'm writing my last chapter and completing my final edit.

A plan to only write 20,000 words and include almost no pictures had grown to 62,000 words and 170 pictures with several accompanying recipes. I also found that I had retraced my youth and many forgotten experiences I had forgotten long ago; a revelation that everyone should experience. It had become a journey within a journey filled with Deja vu.

My hope is that this book and stories will inspire others to engage more during the sharing of meals, purposeful or accidental and expand your own interest and communication skills fostered through the art of cooking. All journeys must end so the next one can begin, therefore I am done. I can't wait to decide which of my dreams will become my next book about people and life's lessons. I have far to travel in the life I have left,

J'ai terminé

CPSIA information can be obtained
at www.ICGtesting.com
Printed in the USA
BVHW090837271221
624881BV00014B/461/J

9 781737 936503